How to Boost Productivity

Work for the Lord

Whatever you do, in word or in deed, do all in the name of the Lord Jesus, giving thanks to God, the Father, through him. (...) Whatever you do, work heartily, as for the Lord, and not for men (Col 3: 17 & 23).

BOOKS BY ADELBERT SCHOLTZ:

Non-Fiction
THE PROPHECIES OF REVELATION
THE THEORY AND PRACTICE OF PASTORAL CARE
HOW TO MANAGE A FLOURISHING CHURCH
EFFECTIVE COMMUNICATION IN THE CHURCH

Fiction
THE ATOM BOMB
THE U-BOAT FILLED WITH GOLD
SHELL-SHOCK
BORDER WAR STORIES
FIVE WARS, FIVE NAMES
THE PROPHET OF PATMOS
TRUST AND DECEPTION

How to Boost Productivity

Productivity Management Done Ethically and Effectively

Adelbert Scholtz

How to Boost Productivity
Productivity Management Done Ethically and Effectively

Copyright © 2025 Adelbert Scholtz. All rights reserved. Except for brief quotations in critical publications or reviews, no part of this book may be reproduced in any manner without prior written permission from the publisher. Write: Permissions, Wipf and Stock Publishers, 199 W. 8th Ave., Suite 3, Eugene, OR 97401.

Resource Publications
An Imprint of Wipf and Stock Publishers
199 W. 8th Ave., Suite 3
Eugene, OR 97401

www.wipfandstock.com

PAPERBACK ISBN: 979-8-3852-5286-2
HARDCOVER ISBN: 979-8-3852-5287-9
EBOOK ISBN: 979-8-3852-5288-6

Contents

Foreword		xii
Preface		xiii
Introduction		**1**
Chapter 1	**The Fundamentals of Ethics**	**23**
	Universal and Fundamental Values	23
	Natural Law and Natural Ethics	25
	Evolution and the Origin of Ethics	28
	Neural Networks Involved in Moral Choices	30
	Ethics and Religion	32
	Ethical Axioms	35
	The Existence of Evil	37
	A Fair Labor Dispensation	39
Chapter 2	**The Ideal: High Productivity**	**44**
	Productivity Defined	44
	Work Behavior as Defined by the Contract of Service	48
	Work Behavior as Defined by the Psychological Contract	52
	The Measurement of Productivity	55
	Productivity and Job Satisfaction	73
Chapter 3	**The Characteristics and Abilities of Workers and their Productivity**	**75**
	Sex, Age, Race and Socio-Economic Class	75
	Abilities and Aptitudes	79
	Personality and Temperament	88
	The State of Health of Employees	94
	Skills and Knowledge	97
	Working Methods	101

Chapter 4	**The Motivation of Workers**	**119**
	Incentives and Intrinsic Motivation	119
	Providing in Physical Needs	121
	Providing in Psychological Needs	122
	Providing in Spiritual Needs	133
	Inspiring Leadership	139
	Attitudes and Interests	143
	Values and Worldview	146
	Self-Concept	150
	Demotivators	152
	Will Power	155
Chapter 5	**Improving the Working Environment**	**161**
	Working conditions	162
	Human Relationships in the Organization	167
	The Culture of the Organization	176
	Pathological Cultures	180
	Policies and Practices of the Organization	186
	Ethical Leadership	190
	The Shape of the Organization	197
	Social Conditions of Employees	208
Chapter 6	**Planning for Enhanced Productivity**	**213**
	Productivity Diagnosis	213
	The Planning Process	224
	A Plan of Action	228
Bibliography		**234**

Foreword

The most valuable asset of any business or organization is its reputation. A good reputation can be destroyed overnight when an enterprise has been tainted with unethical managerial practices.

In this book, the focus is on productivity and on ethical ways of improving it so that an organization as a whole and the lives of all its members can benefit. This represents a timely attempt to cover a vitally important topic and to provide guidelines for employers, management, supervisors, and workers from an ethical perspective.

The author of this book has a vast academic background, very wide experience, and a full perspective on the problem to which he devotes himself here. His extensive experience as a writer and as a scholar enabled him to write a book that is at the same time incisive and easy to read. The result is a piece of work that certainly enhances our knowledge and deepens our understanding of a complex and vexing issue.

Prof Adré Boshoff
Professor Emeritus: Post-Graduate Business School
University of Pretoria

Preface

This book is the result of years of study and personal experience.

The research for my PhD in psychology dealt mainly with the psychology of work. I investigated the work of ministers of religion of the Dutch Reformed Church in South Africa. The goal was to determine whether pastors were doing their work well.

During my time in the ministry, I served three congregations – two in industrial towns and one in a rural area. This exposure gave me valuable insights about the working conditions of factory workers, administrative staff, and entrepreneurs on farms who employ unskilled workers.

With my background in ecclesiastical law, I served on various boards and committees in my church. I acted as an expert witness on church law during court cases.

As a part-time chief chaplain of an infantry brigade of the South African Army, I received training in the management of military units. I observed many military units in various situations, including five shorter periods in northern Namibia and southern Angola during the so-called Border War of the 1980's.

After my retirement from the ministry at the age of 55, I started a new career as counseling psychologist, labor consultant, and pastoral counselor. I am fortunate that my wife has a master's degree in labor law. We often worked together in helping churches, firms, and businesses to reorganize.

Since this book deals with the ethical and biblical principles of productivity management, appropriate biblical texts will be quoted in text boxes where appropriate.

Adelbert Scholtz, Somerset West, South Africa, May 2025

Introduction

THE CHANGING WORLD OF WORK

This book deals with the world of work – the second-most time-consuming activity for most adult human beings. People usually spend more or less 56 hours per week asleep, while they use something like 40 hours per week or more on their work.

The world of work has changed profoundly during the last decade or two in comparison with earlier times. The introduction of artificial intelligence had a lasting impact upon the careers of most workers, directly or indirectly. These changes prompted employers, governments, and organizations to ask: how can we help our workers to be more productive? How can we help them to use their available time and resources more wisely? How can people be aided to work more smartly and achieve more and better results, without working harder or longer hours? Which ethical principles must guide a program of productivity management?

As will be shown in this book, any effort to boost productivity in an organization will encounter difficulties and even resistance and sabotage because the entrenched positions of certain persons may be threatened. It isn't an overstatement to call this a battle to improve productivity – a battle that must be won.

Both my grandfathers would not have been able to

comprehend the world of work of today, while the challenges and opportunities of our time would have sounded like fantastic fairy tales to them.

My paternal grandfather started off in his youth as a shepherd on his father's farm in the Griqualand West region of South Africa. He was, though, endowed with an exceptional intelligence and he taught himself Latin while tending the sheep with the help of a grammar book that he had ordered with the help of the local minister of religion. He succeeded in obtaining some tertiary training in Cape Town and became a teacher during the 1890's. Through self-study he passed the exams to be admitted as a lawyer. He was an exceptional achiever in a time when the only professions open to men were those of the ministry, law, medicine, and teaching. Most non-professional men worked in the government services, in agriculture, or were employed as tradesmen or worked in the retail field.

My maternal grandfather never had the opportunity of studying anything, although he read widely and had an excellent knowledge of the Bible. He remained a farmer and a tradesman (a cobbler) throughout his life, just as most other men during the late nineteenth and early twentieth centuries in South Africa and other parts of the world.

In contrast, my son, who is already in his fifties and has a master's degree in industrial engineering, has already held about a dozen different positions during his career. All these positions were very dependent upon the use of artificial intelligence and he was sometimes in charge of teams of software technicians.

My daughter, who is a few years younger than her brother, is also an industrial engineer. She was involved in projects all over the world, although she lives in Norway most of the time. All these projects dealt with the application of artificial intelligence. Her son is presently being trained as a soldier and a cyber-security specialist in the Norwegian Army – a job that did not exist a generation ago.

The great-grandfathers of my children and grandson would certainly not have been able to imagine these types of careers.

The World Economic Forum has released a report during 2025 with a list of the challenges and problems facing employers and employees in the foreseeable future. This list – in order of importance – must be discussed briefly because any effort to boost productivity must take note of these concerns:

- ***Broadening Digital Access***

Almost all literate people in civilized countries have access to electronic communication equipment and the internet.

They participate in social media, read about world affairs online, do their banking business and perform their jobs with the help of computers and smart phones. The world's dependence upon artificial intelligence is increasing steadily.

Super computers are used to analyze extremely complex situations and make sense of seemingly chaotic scenarios.

- ***Rising Cost of Living, Higher Prices, or Inflation***

This problem is the result of the over-population of the world and the depletion of natural resources. Methods must be found to use natural resources more effectively and economically, and find alternatives. Technology must be developed to use the energy from the sun and other natural forces to lower the costs of electricity.

- ***Increased efforts and investments to reduce carbon emissions***
Mankind is polluting our atmosphere, water, and soil at an unprecedented pace and that affects our health and well-being. All users of implements using oxygen, like motor vehicles, furnaces, and refineries, will have to devise methods to improve the air quality of our planet. More clean electricity must be produced.

- ***Increased Focus on Labor and Social Issues***
The over-population of the world has forced many people from poorer countries to seek a better future in more affluent countries – while the original inhabitants of these countries usually don't welcome these migrants. The rise in the cost of living resulted in demands for better remuneration for work, while employers seek to reduce costs to remain profitable.

- ***Slower Economic Growth***
The economic growth rates of many countries have slowed down and that resulted in the downsizing of the workforce of many enterprises, with the result that the numbers of the unemployed have risen. Many workers were replaced by robots and computers, which do not earn salaries and wages, do not need time off, and can perform their tasks day and night. This resulted in lower production costs, but also in fewer tax payers and less consumers of certain expensive products and services.

- ***Increased Efforts to Adapt to Climate Change***
The legislation of many countries forced enterprises to change to "green" methods of production, which may have affected their cost of production and operation.

- ***Ageing and Declining Working-Age Populations***
The rising cost of living, together with the pressure of over-

population, has forced many families in affluent parts of the world to restrict the number of their children to one or two. That means that the percentage of older people in the population is rising, which creates problems for pension funds, charities, and other social programs.

- ***Increased Geopolitical Division and Conflicts***

The recent past has been characterized by wars in Ukraine, Gaza, Lebanon, Yemen, and elsewhere. There is much tension between China and other countries on the rim of the Pacific Ocean. This creates uncertainty and instability, which must be absorbed by employers and employees.

- ***Growing Working-Age Populations***

Third-world and developing countries are often characterized by a rapid population growth and even a population explosion. That means that the percentage of younger unemployed people is rising, with the resulting social tensions and unrest if they cannot find employment.

- ***Increased Restrictions to Global Trade and Investment***

Some countries, especially the United States of America, are erecting trade barriers to protect their own industries. That causes the overall costs for consumers to rise world-wide because of the extra taxes they must pay for imported goods and services.

- ***Increased Government Subsidies and Industrial Policy***

Trade wars between countries, such as between the USA and China, has resulted in government subsidies for certain products to lower their prices on the world market. This artificial manipulation of prices has warped the economies of those countries.

These trends and tendencies cannot be ignored and their

influence upon the world of work and the productivity of workers must be kept in mind.

- **The Shrinking World**

Instantaneous electronic communication has created the so-called global village where all parts of the world can be reached almost immediately. The internet contains information about any conceivable concept or entity. We live in a world where power no longer relies on force or money, but on knowledge and access to information. We are really and truly riding the Third Wave of the information and knowledge revolution as demonstrated by Alvin Toffler already a generation ago – the First Wave being the agricultural revolution of ten millennia ago and the Second Wave being the industrial revolution of the eighteenth, nineteenth and twentieth centuries.

The fall of the Berlin Wall and the demise of Communism more than two decades ago dramatically highlighted the inevitability of the changes brought about by this Third Wave. Communism and socialism were endeavors to manage and regulate industrial processes from a central seat of power. The knowledge and information revolution, which also swept across the former East Block countries made an economy based on heavy industries and this type of management redundant and it was inevitable that it would fall apart.

South Africa (and any other developing country, for that matter) is part of this new world order, whether we like it or not. We have to compete on world markets and we cannot ignore technological innovations from abroad. If we want to win the war on poverty, we will have to be armed with up-to-date knowledge and technology and participate in the drama of globalization. That means that it is mandatory that workers become more productive.

Organizations will have to adapt to a multitude of variables in a very complex and changing world. These variables include –

- technological innovations;
- economic restructuring;
- the democratization of the workplace;
- social and economic upheavals;
- international political instability;
- increasing shortages of raw materials and rising costs as a result;
- growing need to protect the environment;
- stricter legislation;
- increasing global competition; and
- evolving expectations and needs of clients.

It is imperative that organizations be adaptable and flexible to continue operating. That means that every organization must investigate its shape and structure, built environment, culture, policies and practices, and the way in which its workforce is trained, managed, and led.

AIMS OF THIS BOOK

Although this book is written from a South African background and perspective, it certainly has international applications. There will be several references to the South African situation as an example of the challenges and problems facing many less prosperous countries in the world.

However, the principles, methods and techniques explained in this book are applicable in any underdeveloped, developing, or industrialized country – especially as these principles will be motivated by quotations from the Bible as expressions of universal ethical or moral values and principles.

The purpose of this book is twofold:

- ***First Aim of the Book***

In the first place, the aim is to contribute something towards *solving the huge problem of poverty and unemployment* in many developing countries. Statistics about poverty tend to vary, but nobody can deny that this problem throws a dark shadow over the future. According to Statistics South Africa, for instance, more or less 32% of the employable population in this country are unemployed at any time.

Many jobs were lost since the recession of 2008/9 and the pandemic of 2020. Some experts believe that this figure is actually more than 40% if one takes into account all those workers who have given up on efforts to find a job.

A similar situation is to be found in many other countries. For instance, the unemployment figure for Namibia during 2023 was 36,9%.

Many analysts have shown that the unfortunate high levels of unemployment are one of the main causes for unacceptable high crime rates. Crime costs any country billions every year in direct losses. To this must be added the indirect costs, which include the loss of potential income because the crime rate discourages tourism and foreign investments and the loss of many talented and highly trained young people who easily find jobs in safer and more stable countries.

Introduction

There is unanimity amongst experts that the productivity of workers in a struggling country such as South African is of the lowest in the industrialized world. A UN report found in September 2007 that it takes more than 17 South Africans to do as much work as a single employee in America. This is one of the factors contributing to the problem of poverty in this and other similar countries. It is a truism that higher productivity creates wealth and that a lack of productivity leads to the erosion of wealth. Businesses with high productivity and the resulting higher income tend to grow and expand, which results in the creation of more jobs opportunities.

Laziness and diligence
The soul of the sluggard desires, and has nothing, but the desire of the diligent shall be fully satisfied (Prov 13: 4).
For even when we were with you, we commanded you this: "If anyone will not work, neither let him eat." For we hear of some who walk among you in rebellion, who don't work at all, but are busybodies. Now those who are that way, we command and exhort in the Lord Jesus Christ, that with quietness they work, and eat their own bread (2 Thess 3: 10–12).

One of the factors that determines a country's global competitiveness is the productivity rate of its workforce. The IMD Business School's World Competitiveness Yearbook for 2024 (which looks at the business efficiency and the infrastructure of the countries under discussion) contains a list of 67 larger countries, arranged according to each one's competitiveness index.

Singapore, with its superb competitiveness, is taken as the benchmark and a score of 100 is given to this country. Second is Switzerland with a score of 97.55. The lowest score of 28,85 is given to Venezuela.

South Africa occupies a very low position at number 60 out of 67 with a score of only 46,33. Countries in similar positions are Turkey, Hungary, Botswana, Mexico, Colombia, Bulgaria, the Slovak Republic, Mongolia, Brazil, Peru, and Nigeria. The following countries are also in the bottom half: France, Portugal, New Zealand, Japan, Spain, Poland, and Italy.

In other words: the competitiveness of many industrialized and developed countries is at an undesirable level and in all cases the low productivity of the workforce plays an important role.

That means that the ideas and principles in this book may be applied in most countries in the world – even in the USA with a score of 83,48 at the 12th position in the list.

The competitiveness of a country depends to a certain degree on the cost of labor in that country. Do the workers in a certain country really earn the salaries and wages they are being paid? If the value of their remuneration is higher than the value they add to the enterprise, company, department, or country in which they are employed, their productivity tends to be low.

A 2013 report by Prof Edmund Ferreira of the University of South Africa's Department of Business Management found:

> "Looking at productivity in the country as a whole, statistics show that since 1967, output per worker per unit of capital in South Africa has fallen from R7 297 to R4 924 a year – a decline of 32.5%. From its peak in 1993, this measure of labor productivity has fallen by 41.2%, bringing it down to the lowest level in 46 years. South Africa today is less efficient than many of its emerging market competetors, its labour force is uncompetitive and labour productivity is much lower than that of the rest of the developing world."

Although these words were written more than a decade ago, they are still applicable to the current situation in South Africa – and also in many other countries.

If this trend continues, the economies of many countries are due to run into trouble, since the increase in wages was much higher than the inflation rate and the increase in output – and that will only put pressure on the inflation rate and erode the country's competitiveness.

It is clear that a country such as South Africa compares poorly with other industrialized countries with regards to competitiveness, productivity, and quality of service delivery. The following factors contribute to this lack of competitiveness:

- A sizable part of the adult population (6.76 %) is illiterate or barely literate, having had less than two years of formal education – according to the census of 2012;
- There is a lack of trained skilled workers;
- There is a shortage of people with tertiary education – only 27,17% of adults have more than two years of education or training after having completed secondary school – according the census of 2022;
- There are too few competent senior managers;
- There are too many strikes – In 2024, the Casual Workers Advice Office (CWAO) identified a total of 84 strikes in South Africa, with 45 being wildcat strikes and 39 being protected or legal strikes. During 2023, there were 157 working days lost per 1000 employees with a total of 2 450 317 working days lost and 68 523 employees involved in 2023 as compared to 228 working days lost per 1 000 employees with a total of 3 334 637 working days lost and 153 527 employees

involved in 2022. In comparison, in Germany, 6,4 working days per 1 000 employees were lost due to strikes on average in 2022. In Australia, 99,3 working days were lost per 1 000 employees in 202311; and
- The relatively high cost of labor, which is a result of the low productivity of the South African workforce.

The lazy servant
But if that evil servant should say in his heart, 'My lord is delaying his coming,' and began to beat his fellow-servants, and eat and drink with the drunken, the lord of that servant will come in a day when he doesn't expect it, and in an hour when he doesn't know it, and will cut him in pieces, and appoint his portion with the hypocrites; there will be weeping and grinding of teeth (Matt 24: 48–51).

During 2011, the National Planning Commission in the Department of the Presidency in South Africa gave this diagnosis of the maladies to which South Africa is prone:

"Throughout history many civilizations, empires and countries have experienced dramatic decline rather than progress. The Hapsburg Empire in Europe, Argentina in Latin America and several African states in post-colonial Africa all bear witness to this. The indicators most often associated with decline include:
- Rising corruption
- Weakening of state and civil society institutions
- Poor economic management
- Skills and capital flight
- Politics dominated by short-termism, ethnicity, or factionalism
- Lack of maintenance of infrastructure and standards of service.

"Elements of these indicators are already visible in South Africa, though their strength and prevalence is uneven and differs from sector to sector. If they become more prevalent, the country's progress could be stalled, its gains reversed and even the foundational aspects of democracy unraveled. If these threats are not tackled, the probability of decline will increase."

This warning should not go unheeded – also by other countries in a similar situation. This list of maladies is partly the result of the policy of socialism as pursued by the governing party in South Africa, the African National Congress, as well as other backward countries, such as Cuba and Venezuela. Proponents of this policy try to get all economic activities in a country under government or state control, with as little participation by the private sector as possible. Mines, banks, and industries have to be nationalized.

Experience has proved time and again that this is a recipe for failure because public servants, who must manage all these state-owned enterprises, lack the necessary motivation to make a success of their work since they do not profit personally from it.

According to the IMD Competitiveness Scoreboard for 2024, South Africa lay in 60th position. In contrast, China and India have surged ahead on the competitiveness scoreboard during the last decades since they have abandoned and abolished socialism. India had an economic growth rate of 8,1% in 2005, while China had a growth rate of 9,9% in 2005 – the highest in the world at that time. During 2004 and 2005 China moved up from 31th place on the competitive ratings to 18th place in 2010. During 2024, China occupied the 14th place. India improved during 2004 and 2005 from 50th place to 29th place and in 2007 this country ranked 27th, although India has slipped back to number 31 in 2010.

During 2024, India slipped down to the 39th place – still much higher than the 50th place in 2005.

The main reason for these astounding growth rates is the relative low cost of labor and the resulting high productivity of workers in these countries, coupled with a high degree of training and education in the workforces of these countries. This resulted in many international concerns relocating their operations to these countries to increase their profits. As a result, millions of jobs were created in these countries.

South Africa's labor cost, for instance, is unacceptably high. According to experts, this amounted to an average of $4,93 per hour during 2005. In China, the fastest growing economy in the world, this figure was only $0,75 per hour for the same year. For Sri Lanka, the average cost was $0,44.

The following graph demonstrates that the wages of South African public servants grew out of proportion to their productivity. They were paid much more than the value they produced:

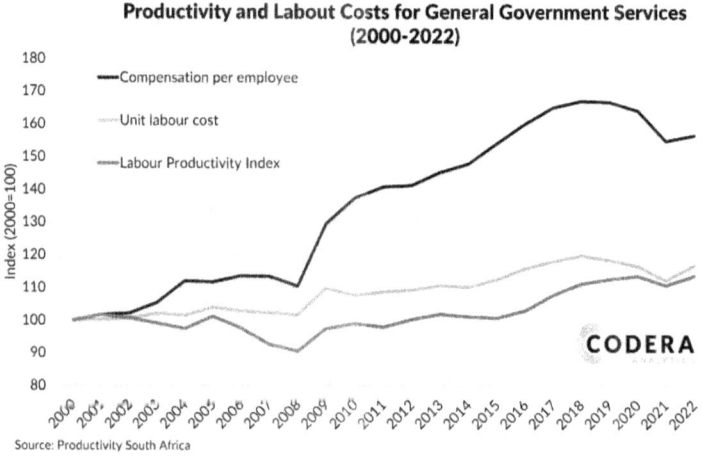

If the productivity of workers in South African and similar countries can be improved, these countries will also become magnets for foreign investments and the accompanying creation of jobs. There is agreement between economic experts that there is a direct relation between the productivity level of a country's workers and that country's general economic health.

A recent study by the research organization Eskimoz has ranked the world's top ten most productive countries by analyzing gross domestic product (GDP) per working hour during 2024. The study selected the 50 countries with the highest GDP per capita and calculated yearly working hours based on average weekly hours. Worker productivity was then determined by dividing GDP per capita by yearly working hours. While not factored into productivity calculations, unemployment rates were included for additional context on labor market conditions.

Here are the top 10 countries where workers generate the most GDP per hour (calculated in US dollars):

- Luxembourg — $146
- Ireland — $143
- Norway — $93
- The Netherlands — $80
- Denmark — $146
- Switzerland — $76
- Belgium — $75
- Austria — $74
- Singapore — $74
- Sweden — $70

South Africa does not even appear on the list of 50 top countries.

Improved productivity pushes up living standards; people with higher living standards are usually healthier people who tend to live longer and who can work more and better. That means that increased productivity is, to a certain extent, a self-sustaining force; where productivity is increased the conditions are created for yet more productivity.

A very large portion of any company's expenses is made up of salaries and wages and in many cases salaries and wages are the single largest items on the budget. If the productivity of the workforce is increased the return on this money is also increased. That means that the profitability of the company improves and the result is that more capital for expansion becomes available. This expansion usually means more jobs. It is generally recognized that job creation is the best antidote to poverty and all the social evils associated with poverty.

One sometimes hears the argument that an increase in productivity leads to a loss of jobs since higher productivity means that fewer people are performing the same tasks that have previously been performed by more people. This argument is only partly valid. It cannot be denied that the productivity of the South African workforce as a whole has been improving over the last decade. This was largely achieved through the replacement of workers by machines and computers – and not by South African workers who were working harder, better, and smarter. The workers who have been retrenched were, in many cases, the least productive workers and that resulted in a higher average productivity rate for the remaining workforce.

Unemployment in South Africa increased markedly over the last decade. During the fiscal year 2003/4, 73 000 jobs were lost; that amounts to 1,1% of the overall number of jobs in the country at that stage.

According to the *Quarterly Employment Statistics Survey* conducted by Statistics South Africa (Stats SA), approximately 8,1 million people were employed in the formal nonagricultural sectors of the economy during the first quarter of 2010. This reflects an annual decrease of 2,9% or about 244 400 shed job opportunities since March 2009. Previously, a further 141 000 jobs were lost in the six months to March 2009.

The official unemployment figure for March 2016 was 26,7% of the workforce – up from 24,5% at the end of 2015. That means that 521 000 workers lost their jobs during the three months up to March 2016. The recession of 2008/9 and the pandemic of 2020 caused a further erosion of employment and the newest rate of unemployment in South Africa show that 32% of the employable population are looking for work. That means that almost one third of the South African workforce can't find employment of some sort.

A very worrying fact is that almost 50% of youths in the age group of 15–25 is unemployed. These unemployed youths numbered almost 2 million in 2011.

According to experts, the main reasons for this state of affairs are the following:

- Socialistic labor legislation that has been introduced since 1995 favors employees above employers and places a heavy burden of duties and obligations on employers;
- Distrust in the policies of the present South African government, which are perceived to be anti-business and socialistic, make many investors wary to invest in South African businesses;
- Uncertainty due to the high levels of crime in this country, coupled with the inability of the present government to counter this trend, has a paralyzing effect upon business;
- In order to stay competitive in the global market, concerns had to cut on labor costs and retrenched

Introduction

several employees – usually the least productive people;
- There is an increasing tendency to make use of subcontractors and consultants and to outsource certain functions, which increases production costs;
- Many trade unions are willing to resort to strike action, with a loss of production as the result;
- There is a tendency for wages to increase more rapidly than productivity; and
- The effect of the HIV/AIDS epidemic on the workplace caused the working lives of many workers to be shortened. That led to a reluctance by employers to invest in the training of people who may not be available a few years later, due to illness or death.

It is clear from the above that the job losses that have occurred were not inspired in the first place by a drive for higher productivity. The job losses were the result of other factors, including the world-wide recession since 2008/9 and the pandemic of 2020. The unintended by-product of these job losses was an increase in productivity amongst the remaining workers.

The example of South Africa was used in this analysis. Similar conditions are to be found in various countries with high unemployment rates and low economic growth rates. The contents of this book may, therefore, be just as applicable to them as well.

By way of summary, it may be concluded that higher productivity leads to improved economic growth and a decrease in inflation. One of the results of that is that more jobs are thus created. Higher productivity may, therefore, also help to create jobs, instead of causing job losses.

If this book can deliver a contribution towards enhancing the productivity of workers in South Africa and other developing countries, then there is some hope that the problems of poverty and unemployment can be contained and reversed.

- **Second Aim of the Book**

The second aim of this book is to *assist employers and managers to boost the productivity of their employees* and thus increase *profits*.

As has already been pointed out, in South Africa, as in many other countries, there are many laws, regulations, and codes that govern the employment relationship. They generally favor employees. The result is that many concerns and organizations suffocate or collapse under the load of over-regulation.

The South African National Planning Commission conceded in 2011:

> "While labor regulations have had several positive effects, most notably the protection of workers' rights, the extension of second-tier social security benefits and the ending of unfair discrimination, there have also been negative unintended consequences. These include making it difficult to sanction poor performers in the workplace, thereby limiting the incentive for firms to hire inexperienced workers."

Some firms downsized their staffs to be less dependent on human labor and mechanized or computerized as many functions as possible. This means that the remaining staff members had to be more productive to keep output at the previous level and to keep the concern afloat. This book endeavors to suggest ways and means to manage and improve these employees' productivity.

It is important to state from the outset that enhancing productivity does not mean that workers necessarily must work harder or work longer hours. That would, in many cases, lead to exploitation, abuse, and unacceptable labor practices. Enhanced productivity simply means that workers must work smarter and use their time, skills, and the employer's resources to greater effect.

This book does not deal with all the aspects of an organization's profitability. It is assumed that products or services are of a high quality, satisfy the needs of customers, and are marketed vigorously. It is also assumed that the latest technology, including computers, is utilized and that production procedures are optimized. Neither does the focus fall on the optimal utilization of capital or raw materials. The only concern here is the productivity of the labor force.

- *Approach of this Book*

Work behavior is a complex phenomenon and the productivity of a workforce is the outcome of many factors, which are usually interdependent. In this book, a holistic or multi-dimensional approach is followed and, therefore, attention is given to all possible factors, which influence the behavior of workers and their productivity and how these factors relate to each other. In the past, most theories or approaches regarding increased productivity tended to concentrate on a single factor of work behavior – with less than satisfactory results.

Some books and articles dealing with a productivity management system restrict their scope to a system of performance appraisal, coupled with a system of remuneration and rewards. Other publications concentrate on better training of the workforce. These approaches are too narrow and do not do justice to a very complex issue. It is clear that a much broader approach is necessary and attention must be given to every possible factor which may have an impact on the productivity of workers.

The factors of work behavior, although numerous, complex, and inter-related, may be arranged under three general headings:

- The characteristics and abilities of individual workers;
- The motivation of workers; and
- The working environment.

These headings form the subject matter of three chapters in this book. Before the various factors that influence work behavior can be discussed, it is necessary to get clarity on the question of what productivity entails and how it can be measured. That is the subject of the second chapter.

The subject matter of this book may be described as the "productivity battle". Productivity management can indeed be seen as a battle that may be won by adhering to the rules and employing a winning strategy.

The rules of this engagement are to be found in the various universal principles and values that define a good working relationship and the labor laws in force. The main thrust of this book is, however, an explanation of the strategies without which the productivity battle cannot be won. The rules ensure that this contest is being tackled in a fair manner. The winning strategies will ensure that the will be won through which profitability will be raised and poverty, low productivity, and a lack of competitiveness will be overcome.

It must be emphasized that these rules must be in accordance with recognized ethical principles. That is the topic of the first chapter of this book.

- *The Intended Readers of this Book*

The contents and message of this book are aimed at the following readers in the private and public sectors:

- Employers;
- Employees;
- Managers;
- Supervisors;
- Work team leaders and foremen;
- Trade union officials;
- Officials of employers' organizations; and
- Students of management and industrial psychology.

This list includes more or less everybody who has some or other interest in the employment relationship and the fate of our financial future.

Chapter 1
The Fundamentals of Ethics

Chapter outline:
- Universal and Fundamental Values
- Natural Law and Natural Ethics
- Evolution and the Origin of Ethics
- Neural Networks Involved in Moral Choices
- Ethics and Religion
- Ethical Axioms
- The Existence of Evil
- A Fair Labor Dispensation

UNIVERSAL AND FUNDAMENTAL VALUES

The subtitle of this book is "Productivity Management Done Ethically and Effectively". It is, therefore, necessary to investigate the fundamentals of ethics and determine how ethics and a religious faith are connected, as well as how ethical and biblical principles ought to shape the employment relationship, especially when productivity management is involved.

Many employers – landlords and factory owners – exploited their workers horribly in the past. The medieval system of feudalism meant that peasants who lived on the estates of noble lords, were compelled to work for these landowners without the option of moving away. During the industrial revolution since the first part of the nineteenth century, industrial workers were often living in abject poverty, while the capitalists, the factory owners, made huge profits.

These conditions led to the French Revolution of 1789, as well as revolutions in the rest of Europe during 1830 and 1848. A revolution in 1917 in Russia led to the fall of the monarchy.

The German philosopher Karl Marx wrote the Communist Manifesto in 1847/48 in which he urged workers to annex all the means of production – factories, mines, and estates. He envisaged a classless society where the exploitation and abuse of workers and peasants would be something of the past and where private property would be abolished. He famously ended the Communist Manifesto with these words: "Workers of the world, unite! You have nothing to lose but your chains".

Communism proved to be just as oppressive as crude capitalism in countries where it was established. It is widely recognized today that both extreme capitalism and communism lead to injustice, poverty, and the exploitation of workers. Many countries have adopted political systems in which the excesses of capitalism were curtailed by the introduction of labor legislation to regulate the relationship between employers and employees, based on certain ethical principles, such as fairness and justice.

Therefore, where this book deals with the world of work, ethical – and biblical – principles cannot be overlooked.

Ethics can be described as the discipline concerned with what is morally *good* and *bad*, *right* and *wrong*. Although the concepts "good" and "right" overlap to a certain extent, they are not identical. The same applies to their antitheses or opposites, namely "bad" and "wrong".

In our time, there seems to be almost consensus that ethics and morality rest upon certain universal, absolute, and fundamental values, which may be regarded as having eternal validity. This approach may be called *absolutism*. Allan describes these approaches as follows:

> "Absolutists maintain that there are absolute moral truths that should apply to everyone because they are universal and operate across cultures and generations. Examples of norm systems that profess to be absolute and universal are the Ten Commandments and, in recent times, the Universal Declaration of Human Rights."
>
> Absolutists "believe that people have a duty to follow certain principles or rules, and most believe that these principles are universal and that people must apply them irrespective of the circumstances and consequences. Certain acts are therefore wrong in themselves and are prohibited, even though they may be morally admirable or morally obligatory."

Reformed theology traditionally took this position. The Heidelberg Catechism declares in Q & A 3 that we can only know our sinful state by comparing ourselves with God's law, which requires from us to love God and our neighbor. In Q & A 91 "good works" are described as those, "which proceed from a true faith, are performed according to the law of God, and to his glory; and not such as are founded on our imaginations, or the institutions of men."

NATURAL LAW AND NATURAL ETHICS

After World War II the absolutist approach with its roots in natural law has won wide acceptance. This became especially clear in key documents, such as the Universal Declaration of Human Rights, the German Constitution (1948) and the South African Constitution (1994 and 1996). Roman-Dutch law, as expounded by Grotius,

Huber and Voet during the seventeenth century, has its roots in the doctrines of natural law. The Constitution of the USA with its bill of rights also rests upon the notion of natural law.

The Universal Declaration of Human Rights (1948), the Federal German Constitution and the South African Constitution each contain provisions regarding universal human rights. Devenish affirms that the thinking of the highest court in South Africa, the Constitutional Court, is also largely based on the tenets of natural law.

Hugo Grotius (1583–1645) claimed that all nations were subject to natural law and he "insisted on the validity of the natural law 'even if we were to suppose… that God does not exist or is not concerned with human affairs.'"

The American Bill of Rights, contained in the amendments to the Constitution, guarantees the following unalienable human rights: freedom of religion and speech, the right to defend oneself by the use of arms, the right to security and privacy, the right to a fair trial and the right not to be punished in a cruel manner.

In the aftermath of the Second World War, when the horrors of the Naz regime in Germany were exposed, the need arose to put the notion of human rights on a more secure footing. That prompted "the desire to invoke rules of right and justice held to be natural rather than merely conventional."

The doctrines of natural law also rest on other notions, besides those of human rights, for instance the rules of natural justice. These rules are applied in courts of law and may be seen as the basis of the whole system of law. This certainly applies to most other sophisticated judicial systems on earth.

The preamble to the Universal Declaration of Human Rights declares a faith in "fundamental human rights, in the dignity and worth of the human person and in the equal rights of men and women", as well as the "observance of human rights and fundamental freedoms." These values are echoed in the first three articles of the German Constitution and in the Preamble and sections 1 and 7 of the 1996 South African Constitution.

The Universal Declaration of Human Rights, the German Constitution, and the South African Constitution are not merely legal documents; they also contain ethical principles and values. The 1996 South African Constitution safeguards in sections 1, 23, 33, and 35 the values of human dignity, freedom, equality, fairness, and natural justice, together with the principles of compassion and care for children and those in need in sections 26–29.

It may be safely said on account of the preceding that the notion of natural law, as well as natural (absolutist) ethics, has won wide acceptance internationally. It is, therefore, possible to discover universally accepted fundamental ethical principles and values, which apply to all people – even to all intelligent, self-conscious, rational, and sentient beings in other parts of the universe, should they exist. Lennick and Kiel in their book on Moral Intelligence state: "We believe that these universal principles exist, even though we know they are not universally applied." They add: "Moral viruses are unfounded negative beliefs that are in conflict with universal principles." These universal and fundamental legal and ethical principles may be seen as axioms or self-evident, rational moral truths or principles.

That the system of government and law must indeed rest upon the principle of *rationality* has been confirmed by the South African Constitutional Court in 2000:

> "It is a requirement of the rule of law that the exercise of public power by the Executive and other functionaries should not be arbitrary. Decisions must be *rationally* related to the purpose for which the power was given,

otherwise they are in effect arbitrary and inconsistent with this requirement. It follows that to pass constitutional scrutiny the exercise of public power by the Executive and other functionaries must, at least, comply with this requirement. (. . .) What the Constitution requires is that public power vested in the Executive and other functionaries be exercised in an objectively *rational* manner." [1]

EVOLUTION AND THE ORIGIN OF ETHICS

Stenger showed convincingly that morality must have had an evolutionary origin. The development and acquisition of moral attributes such as altruism and cooperativeness towards one's relatives and neighbors have been proven through the ages to be advantageous for the survival of the individual and his offspring, as well as for the group to which he belongs.

Shermer shows that the sharing of the proceeds of hunting or gathering in smaller nomadic groups was and is always fair. Everybody got an equal or fair share, even if they did not participate in the hunting expedition or gathering foray. Cheating was unthinkable because the survival of the group depended upon fair and equitable sharing and mutual trust.

Cheating only became possible when mankind became urbanized and the individual could disappear into the multitude. That was the point where morals had to be connected to religion. God or the gods were declared to be the law-givers and invisible

---

[1] Pharmaceutical Manufacturers Association of SA and another: In Re Ex Parte President of the Republic of South Africa and Others 2000 (2) SA 674 (CC) at 709D (own emphasis).

all-seeing inspectors of people's actions in an endeavor to deter cheaters, thieves, and liars from getting away with their evil deeds.

The principle of fairness also occurs in the Bible. It more or less boils down to the golden rule that Jesus gave us:

Fairness
Therefore whatever you desire for men to do to you, you shall also do to them... (Matt 7: 12 – see also Luke 6: 31).

Shermer also refers to international studies of identical twins who were reared separately that showed that moral instincts are largely transmitted genetically. Upbringing and education play a minor role in this respect.

Graffin and Olson declare:

> "Empathy is the best basis for human ethics that we have. It provides a solid foundation for strong personal relationships and a productive society."

Morality does seem to have an evolutionary origin. Lennick and Kiel point out:

> "It is likely that altruistic and cooperative behavior is part of basic human behavior today because it was crucial to the survival of our early human ancestors. People who banded together were better able to master the elements, fight off predators, and acquire food. Individuals who cooperated and helped others tended to live longer. They were more likely to procreate and thereby get their traits into the gene pool. (…) It's not hard to see how the Golden Rule might have evolved – treat others as you would like to be treated – as a practical principle for living harmoniously and working for the common good."

Stephen Pinker declares that higher animals (including humans) are capable of love and care, therefore, prepared to demonstrate altruism and care-taking of others, especially their kin.

Richard Dawkins cites research that demonstrated that normal human beings have a "moral instinct" that works more or less the same in all, irrespective of religious convictions or the lack thereof. This all points to the conclusion: "It's clear we are programmed to be moral."

Shermer points out that a human society cannot survive without mutual trust; the members of the society must trust each other not to cheat and lie if that society is not to disintegrate.

NEURAL NETWORKS INVOLVED IN MORAL CHOICES

The fundamentals of morality are not only being investigated by philosophers and lawyers, but also by neuroscientists.

To behave ethically correct, a person must be able to perform abstract logical and moral reasoning and to choose between various possible behaviors. For that, an intact and fully developed adult brain is a necessity. Our drives often conflict with each other and these may clash with our need to act cooperatively and altruistically.

According to Lennick and Kiel, it has been shown that people with brain injuries mostly "simply lacked the basic neurological equipment to distinguish between right and wrong" and "no amount of education could rectify this." Apart from an intact brain, proper education and nurturing by parents are necessary.

The cortical areas of the brains of children who have not been exposed to good enough parenting and who experienced abuse and/or neglect are on average 20–30% smaller than those of children who have had good enough parenting. There are fewer connections between parts of the brain and without those connections, no empathy is realized, and without empathy, you have impaired morality."

Persons with certain psychiatric disorders, such as an anti-social personality disorder (psychopathy), depression, bipolar disorder, anxiety disorders, attention-deficit/hyperactivity disorder, and autism, often have certain defects in the architecture of the brain because of prenatal or postnatal injury and trauma, genetic defects, diseases during infancy and exposure to noxious substances. These disorders are usually associated with frontal lobe abnormalities or pathology. People with these disorders often lack a moral compass. Likewise, it has been found that people who use cannabis regularly run the risk of damage to the frontal cortex – which impairs their (moral) decision-making ability.

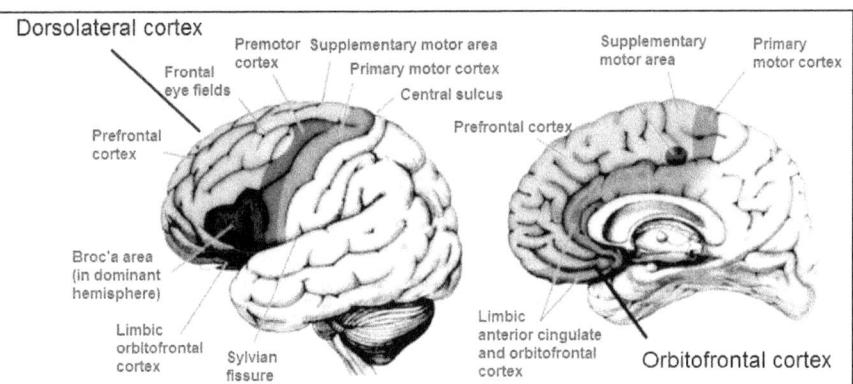

The human brain from the outside and the inside, showing the location of the dorsolateral prefrontal cortex and orbitofrontal cortex. The frontal lobe is the whole area in front of the central sulcus. The parietal cortex (not indicated) is located immediately behind the primary motor cortex and the central sulcus. The cortex is the outermost layer of the brain in which the cell bodies of most neurons are located.

To behave morally, a person needs to experience regret after having done something wrong or bad. That presupposes the construct of a conscience. Brain scans have shown that the dorsolateral prefrontal cortex, parietal cortex, and right orbitofrontal cortex become active when a person experiences regret. (See the illustration to locate these brain structures.)

As with many other cerebral functions, the construct of the human conscience does not seem to be located in a single spot in the brain, but is spread out over several areas.

Primates, including human beings, have so-called mirror neurons in their brains. These neurons enable them to imitate the actions of others and to feel the same emotions displayed by others. This is the neurological basis for empathy – the ability to imagine and understand how another person might feel under certain circumstances. Empathy with its biological basis, therefore, makes virtues such as forgiveness/tolerance and compassion possible.

ETHICS AND RELIGION

Many people think that ethics and religion go hand-in-hand and that without religion there cannot be any morals. This is a fallacy. Buddhism and Confucianism are both Eastern philosophies or religions without a deity and yet they have highly developed moral or ethical systems. It can be demonstrated that the crime rate tends to be higher in countries where the Christian religion has a foothold – especially in those countries where Protestantism is the dominant variety of Christianity. In other words: religious people are not necessarily moral people and people without religion may, in many cases, be moral examples.

In the past, the ethical values and principles of *goodness, fairness, justice, and rightness* were regarded as divinely inspired and formulated by God to endow them with universal validity. For instance, the Ten Commandments has the following preamble, in which God is introduced as the law-giver –

Preamble to the Ten Commandments
God spoke all these words, saying, "I am YHWH your God, who brought you out of the land of Egypt, out of the house of bondage. You shall have no other gods before me" (Ex 20: 1–3).

It must be concluded that the Holy Scriptures, with all their moral prescriptions and ethical appeals simply echo the fundamental and universal values of natural law and a rational approach regarding the differences between good and bad, as well as right and wrong.

ETHICAL AXIOMS

Ethics is a branch of philosophy that rests upon a number of axioms and it is necessary to discover and explain these axioms. An axiom can be regarded as a fundamental and self-evident truth, which cannot be proved, but which is accepted as valid by all people of goodwill.

The concepts of *goodness* and *rightness* are basic or fundamental concepts, which cannot be defined precisely. It is only possible to give synonyms for these concepts. *Goodness* can be described as morally excellent, well behaved. For *rightness*, the following tautological definition may be given: moral correctness. These descriptions or definitions, really, don't say anything. Yet, everybody knows very well what *goodness* and *rightness* mean.

Because *goodness* and *rightness* are such fundamental concepts, one can expect them to be connected to some moral axioms – as will be demonstrated later.

Fundamental and universal ethical principles display the character of axioms or self-evident eternal truths or prescriptions. These ethical axioms have a prescriptive and regulative function and describe how humans ought to behave.

The ancient Greek philosopher Plato already had the insight that there exist eternal ethical axioms – although he didn't use precisely these words. He posed the question whether the gods loved pious and holy people because they were pious and holy or because the gods loved holiness and piety as such. We may translate this question into contemporary language as follows: Does God approve of the actions of good people because these actions are good, or because he approves of goodness as such? This dilemma can only have one solution: goodness, as such, existed from all eternity and may regarded flowing from God's mind.

The most basic question is: which are these ethical axioms? Lennick and Kiel found that there is more or less consensus that the following universal and fundamental moral principles exist:

- *Integrity* Acting consistently with principles, values, and beliefs
  Telling the truth
  Standing up for what is right
  Keeping promises and being dependable

> *Integrity*
> The integrity of the upright shall guide them, But the perverseness of the treacherous shall destroy them (Prov 11: 3).

- *Responsibility*　Taking responsibility for personal choices
　　　　　　　　　Admitting mistakes and failures
　　　　　　　　　Embracing responsibility for serving others

> *Responsibility*
> The soul who sins, he shall die: the son shall not bear the iniquity of the father, neither shall the father bear the iniquity of the son; the righteousness of the righteous shall be on him, and the wickedness of the wicked shall be on him (Ezek 18: 20).

- *Compassion*　Actively caring about others
　　　　　　　Showing kindness

> *Compassion*
> Be kind to one another, tenderhearted, forgiving each other, just as God also in Christ forgave you (Eph 4: 32).

- *Forgiveness*　Letting go of one's own mistakes
　　　　　　　Letting go of others' mistakes

> *Forgiveness*
> For if you forgive men their trespasses, your heavenly Father will also forgive you (Matt 6: 14).

Instead of "forgiveness", one might use "tolerance", which is a somewhat broader concept.

　　This is an elegant scheme. Integrity and responsibility deal with that which is right. Compassion and forgiveness/tolerance describe goodness. These axioms are, therefore, embodiments of the fundamental concepts of "rightness" and "goodness."

There is support for this classification from other sources. Alfred Allan investigated the ethical rules for the practice of psychology in some English-speaking countries and Europe and made lists of the ethical principles contained therein. The following is a summary of his findings:

- Responsibility (5X)
- Integrity (5X)
- Non-maleficence and beneficence (1X)
- Respect for human rights and human dignity (5X)
- Competence (2X)
- Justice (1X)

Integrity and responsibility enjoy wide support as universal ethical principles among psychological fraternities. Non-maleficence and beneficence may be equated with compassion, while respect for human rights and dignity, which also receives much support, may be connected to tolerance.

Stephen Pinker copied a list of "human universals" as published in 1991 by Donald E Brown on account of the investigations of ethnographers on various societies throughout the world. It is possible to classify these universals dealing with morals under a number of headings.

The following human universals may be arranged under the heading of *Integrity*:

- Distinguishing right and wrong
- Law (rights and obligations)
- Redress of wrongs
- True and false distinguished
- Fairness (equity), concept of

- Moral sentiments
- Resistance to abuse of power, to dominance

The following universals may be classified under *Responsibility*:

- Murder proscribed
- Sanctions for crimes against the collectivity
- Self is responsible
- Sexual regulations

The following may be arranged under *Compassion*:
- Cooperation
- Cooperative labor
- Empathy
- Reciprocal exchanges (of labor, goods, or services)
- Hospitality

The following universals may be classified under *Tolerance*:

- Conflict, mediation of
- Good and bad distinction

From this, it may also be deduced that *integrity, responsibility, compassion,* and *tolerance* are indeed universal ethical principles and, therefore, eternal ethical axioms.

John Humphreys remarked that we do not commit all sorts of crimes due to fear for punishment, but because we know them to be wrong. "We have known that ever since we became 'civilized'."

THE EXISTENCE OF EVIL

Many people see life as the continuous struggle between good and evil, right and wrong. They even interpret this as warfare between God and Satan. Since moral axioms don't have the same ontological status as the axioms of mathematics and the axioms of logics, they depend on the free choices of intelligent and conscious beings to be obeyed and realized. People must make a conscious choice to behave in a certain way and, thereby, to do that which is good or that which is right. In contrast, the universe and material world operate automatically and absolutely in accordance with the do not axioms of mathematics.

But people may also choose to do that which is wrong or bad. They may, therefore, promote evil. But evil does not have an independent existence, such as the axioms of morality. Evil is merely the negation or conscious denial of that which is good or right. Evil does not have an independent existence, such as that ascribed to the Devil in Christianity and Islam. The Devil may be seen as the personification of that which is bad or wrong, of evil, but that doesn't mean that evil as such is an independent force in the universe. It is totally dependent upon that which is good and right to exist and it only amounts to a conscious decision to disobey, deny or negate these moral axioms.

is an independent force in the universe. It is totally dependent upon that which is good and right to exist and it only amounts to a conscious decision to disobey, deny or negate these moral axioms.

in the universe. It is totally dependent upon that which is good and right to exist and it only amounts to a conscious decision to disobey, deny or negate these moral axioms.

In other words: the existence of the moral axioms of *integrity, responsibility, compassion,* and *forgiveness/tolerance* only become apparent when conscious and intelligent beings obey the prescriptions of these axioms and reject and avoid that which is bad and wrong. These moral axioms may also be disobeyed or violated and then evil appears as the opposite or rejection of these axioms. Then dishonesty, untruthfulness, irresponsibility, cheating, selfishness, hate, cruelty, revenge, and lack of remorse become visible in the actions of these beings. Evil, therefore, is not an independent force; it is rather a parasite, a moral virus, clinging to the fundamental virtues of integrity, responsibility, compassion and forgiveness/tolerance, sucking the life out of these virtues.

Evil, however, is in a certain sense necessary for the existence and recognition or the fundamental ethical axioms. Goodness and rightness can only become apparent and visible when contrasted with badness and wrongness. Nobody would really understand what integrity, responsibility, compassion, and forgiveness mean if there were no people who acted without integrity, responsibility, compassion and forgiveness and everybody acted automatically in an appropriate and exemplary way.

A FAIR LABOR DISPENSATION

Governments and organizations the world over had to take note of two important documents regarding the world of work: The Universal Declaration of Human Rights, adopted in 1948 by the United Nations Assembly, and the International Labor Organization's Declaration of Fundamental Principles and Rights at Work (1998 and 2022).

Many countries have ratified these documents and have incorporated the fundamental principles thereof into their labor legislation.

It is important to take note of these documents because they are supposed to have a decisive influence upon the employment relationship and all efforts to boost productivity must adhere to these principles.

These principles are called "fundamental" and "universal", which means that they are held to be principles that have general validity. They rest on certain ethical concepts, which are deemed to apply to the whole of mankind. These principles and values are not the result of some or other idealist's thought processes, but must be seen as universally and eternally applicable ethical axioms.

It is necessary to discuss the relevant articles in these two documents briefly:

The following paragraph in the preamble to the Charter of Universal Human Rights is important –

> "Whereas the peoples of the United Nations have in the Charter reaffirmed their faith in fundamental human rights, in the dignity and worth of the human person and in the equal rights of men and women and have determined to promote social progress and better standards of life in larger freedom…"

This paragraph contains the conviction that fundamental rights, which rest upon the values of human dignity, human freedom, and human equality, are universally valid.

Article 4
No one shall be held in slavery or servitude; slavery and the slave trade shall be prohibited in all their forms.

No human being may be held as a slave by anybody else.

> *Bondservants and slaves*
> If your brother has grown poor with you, and sell himself to you; you shall not make him to serve as a bond-servant. As a hired servant, and as a sojourner, he shall be with you; he shall serve with you to the year of jubilee: then shall he go out from you, he and his children with him, and shall return to his own family, and to the possession of his fathers shall he return. For they are my servants, whom I brought forth out of the land of Egypt: they shall not be sold as bondservants. You shall not rule over him with rigor, but shall fear your God (Lev 25: 39–43).

Article 20
1. Everyone has the right to freedom of peaceful assembly and association.
2. No one may be compelled to belong to an association.

This article implies that workers and employers may freely organize themselves into trade unions and employers'' organizations.

Article 23
1. Everyone has the right to work, to free choice of employment, to just and favorable conditions of work and to protection against unemployment.
2. Everyone, without any discrimination, has the right to equal pay for equal work.
3. Everyone who works has the right to just and favorable remuneration ensuring for himself and his family an existence worthy of human dignity, and supplemented, if necessary, by other means of social protection.
4. Everyone has the right to form and to join trade unions for the protection of his interests.

It is taken for granted that every human being has the right to work, to fair labor practices, and to earn a living.

Wages

You shall not oppress your neighbor, nor rob him: the wages of a hired servant shall not remain with you all night until the morning (Lev 19: 13).

Fair treatment

Masters, give to your servants that which is just and equal, knowing that you also have a Master in heaven (Col 4: 1).

Article 24

Everyone has the right to rest and leisure, including reasonable limitation of working hours and periodic holidays with pay.

Workers are human beings, not machines, and they need time for rest and a personal life.

Workers need time to sleep

The sleep of a labouring man is sweet, whether he eats little or much; but the abundance of the rich will not allow him to sleep (Eccl 5: 12).

Article 25

1. Everyone has the right to a standard of living adequate for the health and well-being of himself and of his family, including food, clothing, housing and medical care and necessary social services, and the right to security in the event of unemployment, sickness, disability, widowhood, old age or other lack of livelihood in circumstances beyond his control.

2. Motherhood and childhood are entitled to special care and assistance. All children, whether born in or out of wedlock, shall enjoy the same social protection.

Unemployed persons have the right to be protected and supported. Maternity leave for women is implied.

The Declaration of Fundamental Principles and Rights at Work contains five principles that are so fundamental that they have to be realized even when the country concerned has not ratified the relevant Conventions. These are:

- freedom of association and the effective recognition of the right to collective bargaining
- the elimination of all forms of forced or compulsory labor
- the effective abolition of child labor
- the elimination of discrimination in respect of employment and occupation; and
- a safe and healthy work environment.

Fair labor practices

You shall not oppress a hired servant who is poor and needy, whether he be of your brothers, or of your sojourners who are in your land within your gates: in his day you shall give him his hire, neither shall the sun go down on it; for he is poor, and sets his heart on it: lest he cry against you to YHWH, and it be sin to you (Deut 24: 14–15).

Some of these ideas also occur in the Charter of Fundamental Human Rights. However, the prohibition of child labor, the prohibition of discriminatory practices, and the right to a safe and healthy working environment are new concepts.

Chapter 2
The Ideal: High Productivity

Chapter outline:
- Productivity Defined
- Work Behavior as Defined by the Contract of Service
- Work Behavior as Defined by the Psychological Contract
- The Measurement of Productivity
- Productivity and Job Satisfaction

PRODUCTIVITY DEFINED

Before we can discuss ways and means to enhance the productivity of workers it is necessary to get clarity on the following question: What is the meaning of the word *productivity*? After all, you cannot even try to improve anything if you do not know *what* that something is that has to be improved.

The word *productivity* can very easily be misunderstood. That is due to the fact that this word can be used in different contexts and from different perspectives.

- *Viewpoint of Economics*

From the viewpoint of economics or business management **productivity** can be described as –

output per unit of input employed.

That means, in other words, that productivity is the measure of how much an organization is creating relative to its inputs; if each unit of resources can produce more, productivity increases. Input or resources, in this sense, means money, time, or material.

Three examples may illustrate this:

- If factory A uses 1 cubic meter of wood to produce twenty chairs, while factory B employs 2 cubic meters of wood to produce the same result, it is clear that the productivity of factory A is double that of factory B.
- If factory C can produce a shirt at $100, while factory D needs $200 to produce the same shirt, then factory D's productivity is only 50% of that of factory C.
- Factory E produces 1000 kg of cheese in a day. Factory F produces the same amount of cheese every two days. It follows that factory E is twice as productive as factory F.

Since this book deals with the enhancement of the productivity of workers and not the productivity or profitability of enterprises, this description of productivity will not be used.

- **H R Viewpoint**

In the field of human resources management, *productivity* can be defined as –

> *the ratio between the costs of the worker to the organization and the wealth or value created by the worker.*

The Ideal: High Productivity

It may also be described as an indicator of an employee's *efficiency* and *effectiveness* and it is measured in terms of the products and/or services created per unit of input.
For example:

- If Samantha produces twenty garments per working day and Susan produces only ten comparable garments in the same time, then Samantha is twice as productive as Susan.
- If Jonathan does repairs to motor cars to the tune of $1000 per day and Jeremy's efforts are worth $2000 per day, then it is clear that Jeremy's productivity is double that of Jonathan's productivity.

There are basically six ways to improve the productivity of an organization:

- Improve and provide new plant, equipment, and technology – this is a long-term solution;
- Improve basic production processes and service delivery by means of ongoing research and development – this is also a long-term solution;
- Simplify the product or service range, reduce variety, and concentrate on the core business of the organization – this is a medium-term solution;
- Improve methods and procedures for production or service delivery – this is a short-term solution;
- Improve the planning of work and the use of manpower

- this is also a short-term solution; and
- Increase the overall efficiency and effectiveness of employees – this is, likewise, a short-term solution.

This book is primarily concerned with the last two approaches mentioned in the above list.

Since higher productivity has to do with better efficiency and effectiveness, it is necessary to examine these concepts.

- ***Efficiency and Effectiveness***

In everyday usage, efficiency and effectiveness are often used as synonyms. They must, however, be distinguished from each other. Since we will encounter these concepts quite often, it is necessary to describe them in some detail.

Effectiveness may be defined as –

the ratio of actual output to planned output.

In other words: effectiveness may be seen as the extent to which the goals of the individual or the organization have been reached.

Efficiency, on the other hand, is –
the measure of the speed and accuracy with which work is completed; or
the rate at which input is converted to output.

That means that an efficient worker is not always an effective worker. The efficient worker may work fast and accurately, but that does not necessarily mean that his or her efforts help to attain the goals and objectives of the organization. An example may illustrate this:

Henry is an accountant's clerk and works alone in an

office. Suddenly he decides that his office needs to be painted. He draws some paint, brushes, and tarpaulins from the firm's store and succeeds in painting the whole office in one afternoon. His painting operation may be described as very efficient, but it isn't effective. He worked very well, but he is not being paid to paint, but to calculate his firm's income and expenditure and, therefore, his efforts didn't contribute much to the goals or objectives of his organization and of his position. He may, therefore, be reprimanded by his boss for wasting working time and materials.

In other words:

- An efficient worker works well; and
- An effective worker does the right things.

The productive worker is both efficient and effective. That worker does things right and also does the right things. When you wish to boost the productivity of your workforce, department, or team, both their efficiency and effectiveness need attention.

WORK BEHAVIOR AS DEFINED BY THE CONTRACT OF SERVICE

It is standard practice in the world of work that a written contract of service be agreed upon between every employer and employee. This contract stipulates what each party to this contract may expect from the other party.

The employer may expect that the employee does his or her work according to the job description in the contract of service and according to certain performance standards. The employee may expect to be remunerated for his or her work according to an agreed rate of payment, to receive other benefits and to be entitled to a certain amount of leave.

- *Job Descriptions*

One of the most important clauses in a contract of service is the clause describing the employee's job. This job description must be detailed enough for the worker to know exactly what is expected of him or her. It is desirable that the job description describe how the worker's job relates to the overall goals and aims of the organization. That means that the job description must lay down what the worker must do to be effective.

This job description is in many cases the result of an extensive job analysis. This procedure requires the efforts of a specialist who must examine the needs of the organization, determine the tasks that must be performed to meet those needs and compile a meaningful combination of tasks into one job.

It must be a meaningful combination since it may create enormous difficulties if widely divergent tasks are given to a certain job incumbent who is not qualified to perform such a variety of tasks. These tasks have, therefore, to be related to each other in a meaningful way and support each other. It is the ideal that every job has its own focus and area of operations which must have as its ultimate goal the furtherance of the business of the concern.

A job analysis of an existing job can be conducted in one or more of the following ways:

- The job analyst gets the relevant information from the job holder and/or his supervisors;
- The job analyst observes the operations of the job holder for a certain period and makes a list of his/her tasks; or
- The job analyst performs the job himself/herself for a certain period to ascertain what the elements of the particular job are.

When an organization wants to install a new job position, it is advisable to convene a meeting of all interested parties to discuss which tasks should be assigned to that particular position.

It is not always possible to give a very precise job description in the service agreement since it will be expected of the employee to be able to perform a variety of tasks within his or her field of expertise. This is particularly true of members of a team where the team determines each member's role. In such a case, the job description will have to be couched in general terms.

- *Performance Standards*

It is self-evident that an employee may not be dismissed for incapacity or poor work performance if he or she isn't aware of the performance standards expected from him or her. There is, therefore, an obligation on every employer to communicate the expected performance standards to all employees. These performance standards relate to required output, expected productivity and prescribed procedures. These standards must stipulate –

- how much work or output is required in a certain period;
- how each task is to be performed; and
- how well these tasks are to be performed.

Performance standards must also result from a job analysis. When too low or too high standards are set the organization will inevitably suffer; low standards may result in low productivity, while too high standards will be unattainable with the result that tension between management and workers becomes inevitable.

Job well done
The first [servant] came before him, saying, Lord, your mina has made ten more minas. He said to him, Well done, you good servant! Because you were found faithful in a very little, you shall have authority over ten cities (Luke 19: 16–17).'

It is important that an agreement regarding performance standards be reached between management and employees. Management should state its expectations and employees ought to be given the opportunity to comment on these expectations. Thereafter, consensus is to be sought. This ensures that the employee knows exactly what is expected of him or her and agrees that these expectations are fair and attainable. This agreement may be regarded as an annexure to the written contract of employment, while the contract itself must contain a reference to the agreement regarding performance standards.

    The agreement regarding performance standards ought to be revised from time to time. When new duties are added to the job or when the job description changes over time, it goes without saying that new performance standards must be negotiated.

- *Measurement of Effectiveness and Efficiency*

The job description must be used as a standard to measure a worker's effectiveness. The questions that must be answered are:

- Does the worker perform the correct tasks? and
- Does his or her work contribute to the attainment of the organization's goals?

The performance standards must also be used to measure the worker's efficiency. The questions that must be answered are:

- How well did the worker perform his or her tasks? Does he or she satisfy the performance standards?
- Does the worker perform adequately or produce enough with the allotted time and resources?

WORK BEHAVIOR AS DEFINED BY THE PSYCHOLOGICAL CONTRACT

Apart from the formal contract of service between an employer and employee, there also exists a so-called psychological contract between these parties. This type of contract consists of all the unwritten, informal, and implied expectations and obligations the two parties have towards each other.

- *Expectations of the Employer*

Every employer expects loyalty from all employees. That means that employees are expected not to engage in any conduct which may harm the organization and its reputation or thwart the goals and business of the concern, to defend the practices and policies of the organization and to place their time, energy, and capabilities at the disposal of the organization. In other words, the employer may

The Ideal: High Productivity

expect from all employees to be committed to their work, to be loyal to the organization and that their productivity be optimal.

Employers may also expect to be treated with respect, that their human rights be respected, that their good faith be accepted, that the workers accept the culture of the organization and that the employment relationship be characterized by honesty, openness, loyalty, fairness, and trust.

Loyal service

Servants, be obedient to those who according to the flesh are your masters, with fear and trembling, in singleness of your heart, as to Christ; not in the way of service only when eyes are on you, as men-pleasers; but as servants of Christ, doing the will of God from the heart; with good will doing service, as to the Lord, and not to men (Eph 6: 5–7).

- **Expectations of the employee**

On the other hand, an employee may expect that the employer treats him or her justly and fairly, look after his or her interests and welfare, respect his or her human dignity, respect his or her human rights, trust and accept him or her and be sympathetic towards his or her needs and aspirations.

Be kind towards servants

Masters, give to your servants that which is just and equal, knowing that you also have a Master in heaven (Col 4: 1).

When any party to this psychological contract reneges on his or her obligations, this relationship suffers or breaks down – which makes continued employment difficult or even untenable.

- **Conclusion**

The psychological contract amounts to the following:

- Every employee is legally and morally obliged to be a loyal and productive worker; and
- Every employer is legally and morally obliged to create the conditions to make it possible for employees to be loyal and productive.

The psychological contract between employer and employee rests on the assumption that both parties have the obligation to satisfy the psychological and spiritual needs of the other – these needs being the need for identity, the need for stimulation, the need for security, the need for freedom and responsibility, and the need to find meaning in life and in work.

This book deals with strategies and methods employers may utilize to create the conditions for optimum productivity.

There can also be a psychological contract between a voluntary organization and its members. A friend of mine used to play a leading role in his church. Unfortunately, a quarrel broke out

> *between the ministers of the church and consequently one of them was dismissed. Since my friend defended the dismissed minister and tried to broker conciliation, he was accused of creating a schism. This unjust accusation hurt him to such a degree that he broke his ties with this church and joined another congregation. He declared that his psychological contract with the previous congregation was destroyed as a result of these unjust and unjustified accusations.*

THE MEASUREMENT OF PRODUCTIVITY

Any program to enhance productivity will be useless unless a system for the measurement of productivity is also adopted. If productivity is to be improved, it is necessary that one knows what the current levels of productivity are. Productivity must also be measured on future occasions to determine whether any improvement has occurred.

To determine whether an improvement in productivity in the economic sense did, in fact, take place you simply have to conduct a book-keeping exercise. You need only to determine whether operational costs have decreased and profit margins have improved. This is a relatively straightforward procedure.

This book, however, is concerned with enhancing the productivity of the human workforce. The measurement of the productivity of workers and teams of workers is not always so straightforward since we are dealing with human beings, each with his or her own individuality and limitations.

The evaluation of workers' productivity or performance appraisal is a complex issue that deserves some extensive treatment.

- ***What is performance appraisal?***

Performance **appraisal** may be defined as follows:

> *Performance appraisal is a formal discussion between a supervisor or a panel of observers and a worker or a team of workers for the purpose of discovering how the worker or team is performing on the job and how this performance can be made more effective and efficient so that the supervisor, the worker or the team and the organization all will benefit.*

The appraisal of the performance or productivity of workers is a procedure that has been studied intensively, yet it still poses many problems. That is because the workers who are being evaluated and their superiors, who usually conduct the evaluation, are people and not machines. People are subjective, complex, and variable beings and it is just not possible to measure or evaluate their actions and characteristics accurately and objectively.

No two supervisors will evaluate a certain worker's work performance in the same fashion. That is because each of them has his own biases, value systems, knowledge of the job, dispositions, attitude towards the worker, and perceptions of the job situation. It is also possible that the worker does not perform in the same manner in the presence of certain superiors, depending on his or her attitude towards or relationship with the superior in question.

A great amount of study has been conducted to identify the factors that influence the process of evaluation and to invent methods to minimize their influence. Details of these studies need not concern us here.

- ***The Goals of Performance Appraisal***

The general goal of a system of performance appraisal is to determine as accurately as possible the current level of the effectiveness and efficiency or workers or teams with the aim of improving their productivity. This goal may be subdivided into the following:

  o It must be determined whether a worker's remuneration is in accordance with his or her performance;
  o It must be determined whether a worker or team needs more training and development to perform more productively;
  o It is necessary to determine the level of a certain worker's performance to justify certain personnel decisions regarding him or her. In other words: must the worker be promoted, demoted, transferred, or dismissed, and what are the reasons for that decision? Does he or she qualify for a special bonus or other rewards, and why?
  o The implementation of a performance appraisal system helps management and the workforce to get greater clarity on performance standards;
  o Through a system of performance appraisal management can evaluate the effectiveness of procedures and practices for personnel selection and training programs;
  o A system of performance evaluation can bring to light whether the current workforce is able to do the job properly and whether additional or better trained workers should be employed; and
  o The need of workers to know where they stand in the organization and where they are headed is satisfied through the process of appraisal.

Although no system of performance appraisal is without numerous difficulties it is, nevertheless, also clear that no organization can do without it – especially when management has the objective of enhancing productivity and improving profit margins. It has been found that the presence of a good appraisal practice in a concern is the single most critical factor in any program of productivity enhancement since it creates a culture of performance.

It is important to realize that, although formal appraisals are to be conducted annually or at shorter intervals, informal appraisals should be an ongoing process and be part-and-parcel of the task inventory of all leaders. Managers and supervisors ought to assist their subordinates at all appropriate times to correct mistakes, learn new skills and procedures and to improve their performance. When this informal system of appraisal is in place the formal annual appraisals should bring no nasty surprises for employees.

It is to be recommended that supervisors keep a record of all sessions with those they supervise and the outcome of these sessions. In this manner, a paper trail of all the complaints, mistakes, achievements, instructions, counselling, and praise in respect of a certain worker is created and that helps the supervisor to compile an assessment report at the right time.

> *My late mother used to be a primary school teacher. She loved her work and everybody knew that. The head master, a very kind and soft-spoken man, knew everything that went on in his school and he was very proud of the way she handled her class. As a result he wrote glowing reports regarding her work and gave her much freedom to perform her work in the manner she saw fit. Many years after she had retired, she still longed back to those days because of the way her work was evaluated and appreciated.*
>
> * * *
>
> *A firm in which I was involved with used to have weekly staff meetings for every department where staff members reported back on their output, successes, failures, and problems. Records of these meetings were kept and it was possible to plot a graph for each employee's performance. In this manner, problems could be dealt with timeously and praise could be given for improved productivity and creative solutions for problems could be found. Each department chief reported back to a weekly meeting of department chiefs with the MD where a comprehensive picture of the whole firm's performance could be assembled.*

- **Methods of Performance Appraisal**

A fairly large number of performance appraisal systems have been devised over the years. The aim has always been to minimize subjective judgements by supervisors and to get as near as possible to an objective evaluation of a certain worker or team. Most of these systems and methods have proved to be impracticable, mostly because of their complexity.

There are only two systems that really work:

- **Direct Methods: The Measurement of Outputs**

This is a simple procedure in cases where workers' output can be measured directly and accurately. It is a relatively straightforward procedure to count the number of articles that a certain worker or team has manufactured in a certain period or to calculate how much income a certain employee has generated in a month.

Some examples might illustrate this:

- Workers in a clothing factory each works at his or her own pace. It is simple to count how many acceptable garments each worker produces each day.
- A lorry driver's productivity may be calculated by taking into consideration the distances he travelled in a given time, the time he spent on the road, the number of accidents in which he was involved in a certain period and whether he could keep the operating costs of his vehicle as low as possible.
- The productivity of a salesperson is dependent upon the total amount of cash brought in and the number of satisfied customers who have been served.

This system is not practical in many instances, especially where –

- a job consists of a complex combination of tasks;
- the worker is a member of a team or working unit; or
- the employee renders a service instead of producing a product and works with people or abstract ideas.

> *The recruitment company of which I was CEO used to hold a staff meeting every Monday during which the sales figures generated by each staff member during the previous week were discussed. It was very easy to measure each member's contribution to the overall performance of the company and to measure growth over a period of time. The time was also used to discuss problems and possible solutions to improve productivity.*

- **Behavioral Observation Scales**

This is the method of choice where it is not possible to measure outputs directly. According to this system a rater (usually the employee's supervisor) or a panel of raters judges the quality and quantity of work, as well as the employee's ability to perform the job, on a rating scale. This scale must be based on the employee's job description and on a job specification.

The following types of items must appear on the scale:
- The most important and most crucial tasks to be performed by the employee;
- The type of behaviors that must be exhibited while performing the job (*i e* the methods and procedures to be followed);
- The most important abilities and skills required for the job in question; and
- A list of achievements and mistakes that the person made during the preceding period and steps taken to remedy these mistakes.

The rater(s) must then judge how well the worker performed the tasks mentioned and to what extent he or she has the required behaviors, abilities, and skills. In most cases the judgement is recorded on a five-point scale or a seven-point scale where 5 or 7 denotes work or abilities of exceptionally high quality and 1 denotes work or abilities of a very poor quality. On a five-point scale a score of 3 means performance of average quality. On a seven-point scale a score of 4 denotes the average.

A five-point scale or a seven-point scale usually gives a distorted assessment, since experience has shown that raters rate 90% or more of the ratees as being above average – which is a mathematical impossibility, since only ±50% can be rated as being above average.

Experience has also shown that employers are mostly only interested in the following: are the work, behavior, and abilities of the worker *unacceptable, acceptable,* or *excellent*? A three-point scale with these three anchors is much more easily administered and gives results that are more accurate, since no comparison with the hypothetical and non-existent "average worker" is made.

An example for an assessment form for the work of a teacher might be something along the following lines:

Performance Appraisal of Teachers

Name of teacher: ……………………………………………

Name of rater: ……………………………………………

School: ……………………………………………

Date of appraisal: ……………………………………………

Please rate the teacher according to his/her quality of work and abilities by drawing a circle around the appropriate number in the scale. The numbers have the following meanings:

    1   *unacceptable*
    2   *acceptable*
    3   *exceptional*

Quality of Work

1. How well are his/her lessons or lectures prepared?
     1   2   3
2. How well are lessons or lectures presented?
     1   2   3
3. How good is his/her administrative work?
     1   2   3
4. What is the quality of his/her examination papers?
     1   2   3
5. How punctual is he/she with the execution of tasks?
     1   2   3
6. What is the overall quality of his/her work?
     1   2   3

Behaviors

7. How much love and warmth does he/she give the pupils?
   1   2   3
8. How good are his/her social skills and behavior?
   1   2   3
9. How much interest does he/she show in the personal problems of pupils?
   1   2   3
10. How much understanding does he/she show for the world in which pupils live?
    1   2   3
11. How much time is spent in actual teaching?
    1   2   3

Quality of Abilities and Skills

12. How well is he/she able to motivate the pupils?
    1   2   3
13. How well is he/she able to explain an idea or concept logically and clearly?
    1   2   3
14. How well can he/she ask relevant questions?
    1   2   3
15. How well is his/her ability to listen?
    1   2   3
16. How well can he/she maintain order and discipline?
    1   2   3
17. How good is his/her knowledge of the subject(s) he/she teaches?
    1   2   3

General

18. How many valid and verified complaints have been received regarding this teacher's work and conduct during the past year?
   ....

19. What was being done about these complaints?
   ....
   ....

20. Give a list of achievements during the last year:
   ....
   ....

21. What were the main problems the teacher must contend with?
   ....
   ....

22. How has he/she solved these problems?
   ....
   ....

Total score: ....
General remarks:
....
....

- *Self-Appraisal*

It is necessary to say something regarding self-appraisal.

In many cases, it is not possible for a supervisor to appraise the work of an employee because this work is not performed in an observable or visible manner. Consider the case of a teacher for whom a sample appraisal form has been given above. It is just not possible for the head master to know how well every teacher is prepared for every lesson or lecture. A few spot checks can perhaps be made by attending the teacher's classes unannounced, but in most cases that is not practical. When that occurs, the head master must rely on how the teacher rates himself or herself.

Most workers usually know fairly accurately how well or how poorly they perform. If there is a trusting relationship between the supervisor and the employee it is possible that the employee will give an honest evaluation of his or her own work. Of course, there is always the temptation to present one's own work in a more positive light, but a supervisor who knows his or her subordinates will be aware of this tendency.

To ensure greater honesty the employee must be given the assurance that any information divulged during a self-appraisal will not be used during disciplinary hearings or investigations into the quality of work aimed at possible dismissal or promotion. After all, nobody will be willing to give self-incriminating evidence that can be used later against him or her. The assurance must be given that no record of this information is to appear in the employee's personnel file and that this information is needed for one purpose only, namely the identification of development and training needs of the individual and the organization as a whole.

- *Persons Appointed as Appraisers*

In most firms and organizations, appraisals are being conducted by supervisors and managers who must evaluate the work of their subordinates. This may sometimes create tension between superior and subordinate where the subordinate has the impression that the superior is not being fair or impartial. For that reason, many enterprises have adopted the system of panel appraisals.

Every member of the organization, including the chief executive officer and the managing director, is appraised by a panel of at least four persons consisting of superiors, peers, and subordinates. The aggregate of each rating is taken as the final score. This ensures greater objectivity and less resentment.

This system ensures that the work of supervisors and managers are not only evaluated by their superiors, but also by the people who are being affected by their decisions and actions. In this manner, the quality of their work (and leadership) can be assessed from different perspectives.

The quality of work of senior managers is, very often, evaluated by 'n panel comprised of members of the HR Committee of the board of directors of the company.

It is difficult to assess the work of a team member in isolation because each team member's efforts are dependent on the contributions of all the other members. The solution is to appoint the whole team as an evaluating panel to assess the work of the team as a whole and of each member separately.

Where a team of workers is to undertake self-appraisal, the following procedure may be followed:

- A maximum of six people should convene in a meeting with the object of planning the evaluation;
- The group should reach consensus on the criteria to be used and procedures to be employed;
- The whole team meets to discuss the work performance of every member; that member should, of course, also state his or her case;
- The performance of the team as a whole is also discussed and analyzed;
- This discussion is conducted against the background of the criteria agreed upon;
- The object is to reach consensus about every appraisal; and
- Notes are being kept of the discussions for future reference.

- ***The Procedure to be Followed During Appraisals***

Appraisals usually follow the following procedure:

- Management decides to evaluate the performance of the work force and appoints somebody to conduct or lead the exercise;
- This person decides on a method and a strategy for conducting the appraisal;
- Supervisors, managers, and employees who are to be used as evaluators are given appropriate training;
- The chosen method is applied and its implementation is monitored to ascertain whether this method lives up to expectations;
- Information that is gained is evaluated;
- A decision is taken regarding the method of dissemination of the information; and
- All interested parties – management and employees – are informed regarding the results of their appraisal.

Although it might appear from this explanation that performance appraisal is a relatively straightforward procedure it is not always so simple. In a big concern with a complex organization, it is desirable that a specialist from the personnel department design the process and train supervisors and groups in the art of evaluation. In a smaller concern, where individual employees often have many roles to play, the design of an evaluation process calls for the help and advice of a consultant.

- ***Feedback after an Appraisal***

It is important that employees who have been evaluated receive feedback regarding their appraisal – otherwise the whole exercise would have been pointless. This feedback should be given during a confidential interview between the rater or raters and the employee or team concerned.

The interview should not be used as a witch-hunt where the employee is criticized without giving praise for the positive points in the evaluation. Nor should the feedback be so vague and general that the employee is essentially left in the dark regarding his or her weak points.

The feedback interview is furthermore –

- not an occasion for criticizing the employee's personality;
- not an occasion to blame the employee for mistakes or gaps in his or her make-up over which he or she has no control;
- not a monologue by the rater; or
- not an occasion to put the blame on an employee for mistakes (complaints against employees must be handled at formal disciplinary hearings).

The confidential feedback interview should be conducted as soon as possible after the appraisal. The employee must be given ample opportunity to state his or her case and to give reasons why he or she does not agree with a certain finding in the evaluation or to give reasons for an unsatisfactory performance.

The interview should focus on finding solutions for the problems identified and the employee must have an opportunity to participate in the finding of possible solutions. It is desirable that the employee declare his or her commitment to the proposed solution. Areas in which the employee needs development or further training should be dealt with in the same manner.

The Ideal: High Productivity

It should be stressed that the interviewer must be specific in his or her criticism of the worker. Generalities such as "bad time management" or "lack of concentration" should be avoided. Instead, the worker should be informed of specific occasions when deadlines were not met or when exactly it was apparent that he or she did not apply his or her mind to the task.

It is also important not to criticize the person – only behaviors. It won't do any good to tell a worker that he or she is a "bad influence" in the firm; rather tell the person what he or she did wrong or at which occasion he or she set a wrong example.

The feedback should concentrate on behaviors that can be changed. It is not useful to tell an employee that he or she should have chosen another job. Information and instruction on how to correct mistakes and how to improve performance is much more appropriate. Criticism should, therefore, always be constructive instead of destructive. The person conducting the interview should not belittle or insult the employee, lose his temper, or discuss the employee's defects, faults, and mistakes with others.

Since much must be discussed during the interview it can easily happen that the worker forgets many important points afterwards. It is helpful if a copy of the worker's appraisal report is presented to him or her and that the results of the discussion be summarized and confirmed afterwards in a confidential letter or memo to that worker.

The appraisal interview should be a pleasant event for both the supervisor and the worker. Many people hate it, but that is not necessary. If these guidelines are followed, both parties will experience it as a constructive exercise.

There is a legal obligation on employers to conduct periodic evaluations and feedback interviews with employees. No employee may be disciplined or dismissed for poor work performance unless that employee has received appropriate evaluation, instruction, training, guidance, or counselling. After all, the employer must have convincing evidence that the disciplined or dismissed employee's performance was not up to standard, should the case be taken on arbitration or to a court.

The most appropriate occasion for this guidance and counselling is the feedback interview after an evaluation exercise.

A young man with an engineering degree consulted me. The previous day he was called in for his annual appraisal interview with his supervisor and somebody from the personnel department. It soon became clear to him that these gentlemen did not have any idea how to conduct such an interview. They talked about generalities and asked him whether he had any complaints about his place of work. He concluded that they had no real knowledge of the quality of his work. This experience frustrated him to such a degree that he considered resigning and looking for another job.

Evaluation of the church in Ephesus
To the angel of the assembly in Ephesus write: "He who holds the seven stars in his right hand, he who walks in the midst of the seven golden lampstands says these

> things: "I know your works, and your toil and perseverance, and that you can't tolerate evil men, and have tested those who call themselves apostles, and they are not, and found them false. You have perseverance and have endured for my name's sake, and have not grown weary. But I have this against you, that you left your first love. Remember therefore from where you have fallen, and repent and do the first works; or else I am coming to you, and will move your lampstand out of its place, unless you repent. But this you have, that you hate the works of the Nicolaitans, which I also hate" (Rev 2: 1–6).

- **Requirements for an Appraisal System**

It has already been mentioned that the evaluation of a worker or a team of workers should be handled as a confidential matter. Other requirements are the following:

- The appraisal report should be in writing and must be stored in the employee's personnel file;
- It is necessary that the workers who are being evaluated perceive the system as being fair;
- Every organization or concern should have a written policy regarding evaluation that must be communicated to the employees;
- The system ought to be simple enough for every supervisor and subordinate to understand, administer and accept;
- The system ought to stipulate which rewards, if any, are attached to superior performances;
- Most organizations conduct the evaluation of their staff annually; it may also be desirable to evaluate the performance of a team or task force directly after the completion of a major project as part of the process of reporting to management. It is a good

idea to spread the evaluation process throughout the year and to concentrate on different aspects at different times; and
- The system should be people-friendly and must respect the human dignity of employees.

PRODUCTIVITY AND JOB SATISFACTION

There is a widespread perception that productivity is somehow linked to job satisfaction. That means that many people believe that satisfied and happy workers are also productive workers. This belief is, however, not based on facts.

Numerous researchers have found that there is almost no relationship or correlation between productivity and job satisfaction. It may happen that unproductive workers have high work satisfaction because of the very fact that they get away with the minimum amount of work. Productive workers may, on the other hand, have low job satisfaction because they fear disciplinary measures if they do not perform as expected.

This does not mean that employers may ignore the job satisfaction of their employees. Workers have the perception that job satisfaction is part of the psychological contract between employer and employee. If their need for job satisfaction is systematically and repeatedly thwarted, they may perceive this as a breach of the psychological contract by the employer. The result may be less loyalty and a higher turnover in the workforce.

Job satisfaction is, however, dependent on many more factors than only the working conditions employers create for their workers and adequate and appropriate remuneration. Job satisfaction also depends on –

- the personality make-up of employees;

- the work ethic of employees;
- the appropriateness of employees' training for a particular job;
- the opportunities for promotion; and
- the amount of support workers receive from their family members.

In other words, although employers may be sympathetic towards the amount of job satisfaction their workers enjoy, they have limited power in this regard.

♦♦♦

With this background regarding the nature of productivity and how it may be measured, we can now look at the factors which influence productivity. Knowledge of these factors may help management to enhance the productivity of workers.

The factors that have a bearing on productivity may be divided into three broad categories:

- the characteristics and abilities of individual workers;
- work motivation; and
- the working environment.

Each of these categories is the subject of a separate chapter.

Chapter 3
The Characteristics and Abilities of Workers and their Productivity

Chapter outline:
- Sex, age, race, and socio-economic class
- Abilities and aptitudes
- Personality and temperament
- The state of health of employees
- Skills and knowledge
- Working methods

There are many characteristics of workers that influence their work behavior. It is necessary to know what these factors of work behavior are and how productivity is influenced by these factors.

Some of these characteristics can be changed or developed and others cannot. A person's sex, age, and race, for instance, are fixed. Although one cannot do anything in this regard, it is necessary to know how they interact with work behavior. Where a characteristic can, though, be changed or developed, employers should know how to do this and what their obligations and duties (if any) in this respect are.

SEX, AGE, RACE AND SOCIO-ECONOMIC CLASS

- *Discrimination and Differentiation*

It isn't possible to change the sex, age or race of any person. These characteristics are given and every employer must accept them.

Article 7 of the Universal Declaration of Human Rights

states: "All are equal before the law and are entitled without any discrimination to equal protection of the law. All are entitled to equal protection against any discrimination in violation of this Declaration and against any incitement to such discrimination."

This means, inter alia, that no employer may discriminate against employees and applicants for employment on the grounds of, amongst others, sex, race, or age. That means that no employer may prefer certain employees or applicants above others for appointment, rewards, promotion, demotion or disciplinary action because of their sex, race, or age – except where the inherent requirements of the job call for such action.

Two examples may illustrate this:

- If a business man decides to employ a woman of the age of twenty as salesperson and not a woman of forty who also applied for the job, although the older person is better qualified to do the job, it amounts to discrimination based on age. That is not acceptable and may be contested in court.
- Senior personnel tend to be older people. This state of affairs is not discriminatory against younger people since a senior position usually requires a certain amount of experience and older people mostly have more experience than younger people. The appointment of an older person in a supervisory or management position, therefore, is not discrimination against the younger and less experienced candidates.

Whilst it is wrong and prohibited to discriminate against employees, managers, and supervisors will act wisely if they consider the differences that exist between people of different sexes, age groups or racial groups.

> *A woman in her forties turned to me for help after her application for a certain position was unsuccessful and a much younger and less experienced woman was appointed. It turned out that this younger woman was the girlfriend of the managing director's son. My client was so aggrieved over this discrimination that she took the case to the Labor Court in South Africa. Although the Court only awarded her the costs of the case and nothing more, she was satisfied that this case of discrimination and nepotism was brought to light.*

Although discrimination against women for being women is unacceptable and they must be treated in the same way as their male colleagues, it must be remembered that women have a different style and approach to their work. They, for instance, give more attention to smaller details and the feelings of others – while men mostly concentrate on the overall picture and on the task on hand. Employers must make allowances for this fact if they wish to avoid trouble.

Discrimination based on race is wrong. Nevertheless, managers should know people from different population groups have different cultural roots and therefore different value systems. Their attitude towards their work may differ and different aspects of their work may be important to them. If managers ignore this fact, they are bound to run into problems.

It is not allowed to discriminate against people because of their age. However, supervisors should acknowledge the fact that people from different generations have different attitudes, interests, and value systems.

In other words: although discrimination is wrong and prohibited it is necessary to differentiate between workers to approach each of them in a humane way and by acknowledging and respecting individual differences. In this way each worker's unique talents, abilities and skills may be utilized optimally.

- *Social mobility*

Every person belongs to a certain socio-economic class. This characteristic can be changed to a certain extent. The attainment of a university degree and therefore the improvement of a person's earning power tends to shift that person from one social class into another.

Management should be aware of the class to which an employee belongs since this may influence his or her attitude towards work and the organization in which he or she works. Management should also be aware of the effect that promotion may have on a person's class membership and therefore his or her value system.

> *A man I knew well was not an acceptable spouse for his wife according to his in-laws since he did not earn enough and came from a relatively humble background. He had guts, though. He studied after hours and gained a degree in commercial subjects.*

> *He was promoted in his job, his income rose and he and his family could move into a bigger house. After this, he was accepted by his in-laws as a suitable member of the family!*

ABILITIES AND APTITUDES

It is common knowledge that the abilities and aptitudes of workers have a profound influence on their work behavior and the levels of their performance.

- *Aptitudes*

Aptitudes are –

> *more or less stable attributes of people that relate to their ability to perform certain tasks.*

Many of these aptitudes are inherited and cannot, therefore, be altered. There is no unanimity amongst psychologists as to the number or the precise nature of aptitudes, but that does not deter attempts to measure aptitudes and to relate these to certain types of jobs.

Most researchers would agree that an accountant, engineer, or statistician needs a high score in a test for measuring numerical aptitude. It is likewise acknowledged that a journalist, priest, or social worker must have a good verbal aptitude and that a lawyer must have an aptitude for logical reasoning.

Apart from aptitudes relating to verbal, numerical, and logical faculties, some experts feel that we also have to take into consideration the following aptitudes – or lack thereof: the abilities to be creative, to handle spatial relationships, to handle social relationships, to make sense of the input of the senses, to communicate accurately and effectively and the ability to control bodily movements.

Intellectual ability, as described by an intelligence quotient (IQ) score, is usually included in a list of aptitudes. This aptitude is usually described as –

> *the ability to grasp new concepts, to learn, to reason and to remember.*

- ***Psychological Tests for Determining Aptitudes***

Nowadays many big employers, as well as certain employment agencies, screen job applicants by measuring their aptitudes and abilities – apart from taking their qualifications and experience into consideration. There are several sophisticated psychometrical instruments available by means of which a psychologist can make a fairly accurate assessment of a person's most important aptitudes.

All psychometric instruments used during the selection process must comply with the stipulation that psychological tests have to be reliable, valid, and fair to all cultural groups. Most tests developed by reputable organizations comply with these requirements. The legislation of most countries requires that only a trained and registered psychologist is allowed to administer, score and interpret psychological tests and communicate the results to interested parties.

It is necessary to select the best or most suitable applicants for a job since it is difficult and even expensive to dismiss unsuitable or incompetent workers. Employers are, therefore, advised to select job applicants very carefully with the help of appropriate psychometric instruments before any appointments are made.

No organization can afford to be burdened with incompetent employees. Productivity will inevitably suffer, while those workers will surely experience stress and unhappiness when they cannot deliver the desired results and satisfy the demands placed upon them.

Unfortunately, the prescriptions of the Employment Equity Act in South Africa regarding the preference to be given to black applicants have resulted in a shortage of suitably qualified black persons. Few organizations can procure enough black employees for the middle and higher echelons to satisfy their employment equity plans and fulfill the required quotas. The result is that many unsuitable black applicants are hired. This resulted in lower productivity for the individuals concerned, as well as high levels of frustration and stress for these employees since they cannot attain the required performance standards.

Although the Employment Equity Act has a laudable goal, namely the redress of past wrongs, the introduction of a system whereby firms must satisfy certain racial quotas has been detrimental to the aim of improving the productivity of the South African workforce. Surely, isn't it now the time for this act to be amended?

- *Dismissal of Incompetent Employees*

In the previous chapter, some guidelines were given for the implementation of a system of performance appraisal and it was mentioned that workers' abilities and skills should also be evaluated, apart from their work output or quality of work. Where it becomes plain that a certain worker's productivity is low because of an inability to do the job then it is advisable that management transfer that worker to a position for which he or she is more suitable. If that is not possible, demotion or dismissal on the grounds of poor work may be the only alternative, although that may be an expensive, emotional, and time-consuming exercise.

To avoid the appointment and eventual disappointment of dismissing unsuitable or incompetent workers, it is advisable that management do a thorough job analysis before a vacant position is advertised. This analysis must result in more than simply a list of duties expected of the job incumbent and the performance standards required, but must also include a thorough analysis of the required training, experience, skills, abilities, and aptitudes. There must, in other words, be clarity on exactly what type of person is needed before any appointment can be made.

> *A former client of mine was dismissed from his job on the grounds of purported incompatibility with his four colleagues with whom he had to work together as members of a team. There were complaints that he interfered with the work of his colleagues and that he did not perform all the tasks expected of him. He took his case to the South African Labor Court where it was found that the unpleasant relationship between him and his colleagues resulted from the failure that no proper job analysis was done before he was appointed. The elements of his hastily compiled job description were all those tasks which his former colleagues did not like and a new position was created into which all these unwanted elements were dumped. The friction between him and his colleagues resulted from the fact that his job overlapped with those of his colleagues and they interpreted his honest endeavors to perform his work as interference and trespassing onto their domains.*

- **Development of Abilities**

It is, of course, also possible to develop the abilities and aptitudes of employees to create workers who are more productive. Most people think of intelligence and aptitudes as fairly static characteristics; people are born with them and therefore they are not prone to change. This is, however, not the full truth.

Although a significant portion of a person's abilities and aptitudes are inherited, another significant portion may be developed and increased by appropriate stimulation and training. Specialist educators and/or psychologists may take charge of this process.

Although employers usually do not see it as their duty to improve and develop the abilities and intelligence of their employees, it may prove to be a very profitable undertaking to do exactly that. Sending employees on courses and programs may remove them for a few days from work but the dividends will surely prove to be more than worthwhile.

The knowledge, experience, and skills of employees should be seen as part of the assets of a company. Traditionally, assets were only seen as tangibles such as capital, equipment, tools, vehicles, real estate, and buildings. There are, however, also intangible assets such as good relationships with clients, a positive public image, and the abilities and skills of members of the organization.

It makes sense to protect and develop the valuable asset of employees and their abilities. Employees may have the following valuable capabilities and abilities:

- Knowledge: of the job, of the organization and of the environment;
- Experience: having the know-how from having done the job in the past;
- Motor skills: the ability to manipulate and handle objects such as tools, vehicles, and equipment;
- Perceptual skills: the ability to gather information through the senses and interpret it;
- Cognitive or intellectual skills: the ability to grasp new concepts, to reason, to be creative and to make decisions;
- Communication skills: the ability to receive or transmit messages (verbal and non-verbal) accurately and effectively;
- Social and interpersonal skills: the ability to collaborate productively with others (colleagues, managers, staff, suppliers, and clients) and to fit into a team, department, or section; and
- Values and attitudes: being motivated to do the job and to do it well, as well as loyalty to the team and the organization.

- *The Need for Innovators and Creative People*

In the fast-changing world in which we live, no concern can survive without constant innovation and renewal. Stagnation means certain death. It is, therefore, extremely important to have innovators on the staff.

Innovators have the ability to be creative and see possibilities and challenges where others only see problems. They find novel solutions to old dilemmas and can create shortcuts which may result in savings.

Innovators may be recognized by the following qualities:

- They usually have excellent aptitudes;
- They are well-trained and well-educated;
- They have wide experience;
- They are multi-skilled;
- They are inquisitive, independent, highly motivated, willing to take risks and to persevere in what they have started; and
- They are task-oriented and willing to take responsibility.

It will always be worthwhile to be on the look-out for innovators; they can increase the value of the workforce. If you cannot get hold of innovators, the next best is to have staff members who can grasp new innovations and applying them in practice.

- ***Dismissal of Superfluous Workers***

The productivity of many organizations suffers because they are over-staffed.

It is not so easy to determine exactly when and to which extent an organization has too many workers. It is a law of nature that a vacuum tends to be filled. This also applies to the workplace. When there are too many workers, they somehow succeed in inventing tasks to keep busy and to fill empty hours.

A thorough analysis of the profitability of a concern and a thorough job analysis of every position will show which positions may be declared superfluous and, therefore, made redundant. It must be determined which workers contribute most to the attainment of the goals of the organization and which workers contribute little or nothing.

One of the contemporary buzz words is 'outsourcing'. This

practice certainly makes sense. In many cases certain tasks can be performed more efficiently and cost-effectively by outsiders, by consultants or contractors. It pays to outsource certain functions to these people instead of employing staff to do these jobs. These consultants or contractors are usually specialists in their fields and they may have better equipment and technology at their disposal. Since they work for themselves, they are better motivated than regular employees and do not need constant supervision.

Many organizations have found that a reduced workforce produces much more than the previous over-inflated workforce, simply because many irrelevant or unimportant tasks were eliminated. In addition, a reduced workforce costs less in terms of remuneration and other benefits.

An exercise of reducing the workforce must have the goal of retaining the most competent, most experienced, and most productive workers. This can only be determined if a system of performance appraisal is in place and these workers can be thus identified.

It is acceptable to get rid of superfluous workers on the grounds of operational requirements. The correct procedures as prescribed in each country's labor legislation will have to be followed. That usually means that trade unions or other representatives of the workers should be consulted, that all alternatives to dismissal be investigated, that all representations from the trade unions or other representatives of the workers be considered and that the workers who are to be dismissed be selected in a fair and objective manner. Such a fair and objective criterium may well be that the least productive and the least competent workers are selected for redundancy.

Downsizing the organization may sometimes, unfortunately, result in a crisis of trust in the organization.

The Characteristics and Abilities of Workers and their Productivity

The remaining workers may feel threatened after a downsizing exercise since they do not know whether their positions will be the next to go. It may be traumatic to take leave of colleagues and friends with whom strong ties have been forged over some years and their pain and dismay for being retrenched and becoming unemployed will be blamed on management which is perceived to be heartless, brutal, and ruthless.

For this reason, any endeavor to downsize must be treated with the greatest care and circumspection. It is advisable to act on the advice of experts in this regard.

A relative of mine was recently shocked by the way a downsizing exercise was conducted by his employer. When the previous chief executive officer of his division retired an outsider was appointed by top management with the express task of getting rid of the "old wood" in that division. A few weeks after assuming his new position, the new CEO called a meeting of all his staff members. Without any preparation, he gave them two days each to prepare a memorandum about why the organization should retain their services. Many of the senior and most experienced staff members felt so insulted by this attitude that they resigned on the spot. That resulted in a crisis since more people left the division than was envisaged and much-needed experience and skills were lost. The morale under the remaining staff members sank to an all-time low.

PERSONALITY AND TEMPERAMENT

Another attribute of a worker that is more or less stable is his/her personality and temperament.

- *A Description of Personality*

Although the use of the term *personality* is common in everyday usage, its meaning is somewhat nebulous and it must be defined more precisely. **Personality** may be described as –

> *the totality of all the physical, psychological, and spiritual attributes of an individual that determines behavior and interaction with the environment.*

The term *temperament* is usually used of the way a person handles the emotional side of his or her personality. Some persons display more feelings than others or are more easily emotionally aroused than others and the concept *temperament* is used for this aspect of personality.

It must be remembered that a person's personality must be seen as a totality and a unity. Certain aspects of personality may be distinguished or differentiated but they can never be studied in isolation. The term *personality* is sometimes used for the person himself or herself and then the human being as a whole is meant.

A person's personality can be discerned or inferred when that person acts or interacts with his or her environment. Then certain enduring behavioral patterns, attitudes and characteristics become apparent. These characteristics are not attributes in a physical sense (as the color blue may be a characteristic of a flower or a certain mass may be a characteristic of a stone), but must be seen as the usual way in which that person handles certain situations or relationships.

Although psychologists endeavor to 'measure' certain personality traits, these measurements are only fairly accurate approximations. Psychometric tests are never 100% reliable and valid. Such tests are, nevertheless, very useful for comparing individuals and predicting future behavior.

There is no unanimity as to the number of personality traits that people exhibit. Different personality tests and questionnaires focus on different traits or characteristics. The well-known 16 PF personality questionnaire presupposes sixteen personality factors. Other researchers are of the opinion that personality can be adequately described by the following five dimensions:

- Extroversion – introversion;
- Emotional stability – immaturity;
- Acceptability – unacceptability;
- Reliability – unreliability; and
- Intellectual ability.

Some personality characteristics display a high correlation with success in certain jobs, while others play virtually no role. For example, a salesperson or a teacher must have an extroverted personality since that person needs to be outgoing and make contact with other people easily, while extroversion or introversion plays no role in the productivity of a scientific researcher or an accountant.

- ***Selection of Candidates***

Before a vacant position can be filled it is advisable that management determine through a thorough job analysis what type of personality is needed for a particular job. That profile must then be used as the basis on which a suitable candidate is selected for the job in question and psychometric instruments may be used very profitably towards that goal.

If this procedure is not followed, an unsuitable candidate may easily be appointed – with all the unpleasant and undesirable repercussions resulting from such a mistake.

It certainly pays to have a rigorous selection system in which the aptitudes, abilities, and skills of prospective employees are being assessed since such a selection system will weed out persons who will prove to be disappointments later and who may cost the company a lot of money by being unproductive, incompetent, and negligent. It is a truism that the higher the positions in the corporate structure are, the more rigorous the selection procedures must be since people in higher positions tend to have more and greater responsibilities than those lower down.

Apart from the fact that somebody with an unsuitable personality may not be as productive as he or she could be, that person may disrupt the efficiency and effectiveness of a whole team or task force by reacting in inappropriate ways to situations and relationships. The result may be unnecessary violent conflict and unpleasant feelings in such a group – with the result that productivity suffers.

From the preceding it follows that it is necessary to select the right appointee for a certain job to promote the productivity of the concern.

The selection and appointment process usually includes the following steps:

- A detailed job analysis and evaluation to identify the tasks connected to the job in question, the skills, aptitudes, training, and experience needed for the position and the remuneration package that has to go with the position;

> *Job analysis of an overseer*
> This is a faithful saying: if a man seeks the office of an overseer, he desires a good work. The overseer therefore must be without reproach, the husband of one wife, temperate, sensible, modest, hospitable, good at teaching; not a drinker, not violent, not greedy for money, but gentle, not quarrelsome, not covetous; one who rules his own house well, having children in subjection with all reverence; (but if a man doesn't know how to rule his own house, how will he take care of the assembly of God?); not a novice, to avoid being puffed up and falling into the condemnation of the devil. Moreover he must have good testimony from those who are outside, to avoid falling into reproach and the snare of the devil (1 Tim 3: 1–6).

- Advertising the vacancy – internally and/or externally – and inviting suitable candidates to submit applications and CV's;
- Screening the CV's to identify possible suitable candidates;
- Contacting referees mentioned in the application letters of the most suitable candidates;
- Verifying the qualifications and experience of the most suitable candidates;
- Invitations to the top five to seven candidates to attend selection interviews;
- Selection interviews by a selection panel;
- The administering of suitable psychometric instruments and/or sending the candidates to an assessment center;
- Requiring the candidates to perform certain tasks connected to the job in question or simulation exercises to evaluate their success in completing these tasks;

- The selection decision by management; and
- Making a job offer to the most suitable candidate.

It has been found that the results of an assessment center are the best predictors of future job success. Next in line are the performance of job samples and psychometric tests. Selection based solely on biographical details, references and unstructured interviews are poor indicators of future job success. Graphology, astrology, and palmistry have no predictive value at all.

A good selection process is not only designed to identify the best candidate for a certain job; it is also an opportunity for the candidate to have a look at the prospective employer and decide whether he/she will fit in with the corporate culture and whether the job content will be to his/her liking. When both parties – prospective employer and prospective employee – seem to like each other, it is likely that the job offer will be accepted.

As a member of the Council of the University of Stellenbosch and as vice chairman of the Institutional Forum of this university, it has been my privilege to take part in the selection and appointment of a new rector, four vice rectors and several deans of faculties. Since these positions are crucial for the continued well-being of the university the selection process could not be rushed and it usually took a few months between the job analysis done by the selection committee and the eventual appointment. Most of the steps mentioned above were performed in the selection of the most suitable candidates who would be invited for interviews.

Selection of suitable warriors with a performance test
So he [Gideon] brought down the people to the water: and YHWH said to Gideon, "Everyone who laps of the water with his tongue, as a dog laps, him shall you set by

> himself; likewise everyone who bows down on his knees to drink." The number of those who lapped, putting their hand to their mouth, was three hundred men: but all the rest of the people bowed down on their knees to drink water. YHWH said to Gideon, "By the three hundred men who lapped will I save you, and deliver the Midianites into your hand; and let all the people go every man to his place" (Judg 7: 5–7).
>
> [*Note*: the performance test determined vigilance versus carelessness.]

- ***Development of Personality***

Although personality is a fairly stable set of characteristics it is, nevertheless, possible for people to change – especially to change their habits and style of social interaction.

More and more enterprizes make the discovery that it pays to get psychological help for troubled employees. More will be said on this topic in chapter 4.

One of the objects of therapeutic counselling or psychotherapy is to teach people appropriate ways of dealing with other people or difficult situations.

One of the objects of therapeutic counselling or psychotherapy is to teach people more appropriate ways of dealing with other people or difficult situations. This may help and develop a person who habitually clashes with fellow workers or who does not fit into a team or a department.

THE STATE OF HEALTH OF EMPLOYEES

It is self-evident that unhealthy workers cannot be productive workers. Somebody who is chronically ill and often goes on sick leave, who suffers from pains and low energy levels, or who is not in a physically fit condition is just not able to be productive.

It is legal and admissible in most countries to dismiss workers because of ill health. This is, though, not an easy option since a complex procedure is usually called for in such cases. It may also be a costly option because the appointment of replacement workers may cause substantial expenditures in recruitment, selection, and training.

- *Health Program*

For these reasons, many organizations do their utmost to keep their workers healthy. Measures to attain this goal include –
  o a cafeteria where nutritious meals are served (either free of charge or at a reduced/subsidized price);
  o awareness programs regarding various health issues;
  o subsidized membership to medical aid funds; 'Compulsory annual medical examinations paid for by the employer;
  o a clinic where workers may get first aid and medical treatment;
  o the provision of sports amenities; and
  o subsidized or free membership of a gymnasium or health club.

Many behavioral problems, which may affect a worker's performance adversely, are health-related. It is nowadays acknowledged that some psychological problems such as certain forms of depression, obsessive-compulsive behavior, hyper-activity, aggression, irrational fears and even schizophrenia are at least partly due to dietary deficiencies. It, therefore, makes sense to provide nutritious meals and other health assistance.

In cases where management implements these types of measures workers obtain the perception that management cares for them and therefore they are more willing to fulfil their obligations under the psychological contract between employer and employee.

- *Medical Testing*

It is advisable to appoint healthy job applicants. A job analysis that results in a job description and job specification will usually demonstrate that good health is an inherent requirement for a certain job. Therefore, the medical testing of applicants for employment in those cases will be justified. Of course, it is necessary that the person gives written permission that he or she may be tested by a medical practitioner or another healthcare professional.

It is self-evident that a blind person or a person with a missing limb will not be able to work as a security guard or a truck driver. Such persons may, however, easily be employed in certain job categories where these disabilities are no impairment. Good eyesight is a prerequisite for a driver. Before employing a job candidate for such a position, it should be to have that person's eyesight tested.

It will be positively dangerous to the health of the whole workforce of an organization to employ somebody with a contagious disease such as tuberculosis. Therefore, it is necessary to identify such persons beforehand by means of medical testing.

The medical testing of an employee or applicant for employment to determine that person's HIV status is prohibited in certain countries. This is to prevent discrimination against persons who are HIV positive. The rationale behind this prohibition is the fact that people who are HIV positive are not necessarily ill and are, therefore, able to perform a day's work.

AIDS, which results from the HI virus, is not contagious when certain precautions are taken. In certain jobs, such as in health care, where the virus may be easily transmitted to members of the public or to other workers, it may be necessary to obtain a court order to permit the testing of the HIV status of employees.

While the world still eagerly awaits a cure or vaccine for AIDS, we have the sad situation that somebody who is HIV positive has a limited life span. This means that a worker who is HIV positive will be able to be productive only for a limited period. There are already several industries or labor sectors in many countries where the turnover of workers due to incapacity or death because of AIDS is unacceptably high. It proves difficult to train enough replacements for those workers who become ill or die. Because of this, many companies have replaced a number of workers by machines and computers.

SKILLS AND KNOWLEDGE

Somebody without any skills and knowledge is unemployable. Every job, even a so-called unskilled job, calls for certain skills and an amount of training.

Some of the reasons why the South African workforce has a low productivity rating are the following:

- A large percentage of adult South Africans ($\pm 34\%$) are illiterate or barely literate;
- The South African educational system is largely dysfunctional; and
- Too little attention is given to mathematics, science, and technology in the South African school system.

These reasons apply to most developing countries.

The responsibility for the training of workers rests with more than one institution. The educational system of the country must provide basic skills such as computing, calculating, and communicating. Universities, technical colleges, and other training facilities provide vocational training.

Employers also provide training, which may be formal or informal. Informal training is known as on-the-job-training and in most cases consists of a mentor who instructs a novice. Formal training may take the form of official courses or the provision of bursaries for training at an educational institution.

- *Mentoring*

When an organization wants to utilize a mentorship system it must be well planned. Prospective mentors must be chosen diligently and trained to fulfil their roles.

The following qualities and skills are required of a mentor:

- Good listening skills;
- Good and clear communication skills;
- Willingness and ability to help with the solution of the trainee's problems;
- Knowledge of formal and informal networks in the organization;
- Knowledge and experience of the work;
- Willingness and ability to share knowledge and experience;
- The ability to give constructive criticism and feedback; and
- Respect for the privacy and human dignity of the trainee.

It is important to agree to a clear role division, although the parties must accept each other as equals and a parent-child relationship must be avoided. A clear contract between the parties ought to be include stipulations about who does what, how long the relationship is to last, how progress will be evaluated, how the relationship is to be nurtured, a code of conduct and the availability of the mentor. The goal must always be the development of the trainee and the trainee must be willing to accept the leadership of the mentor.

- ***Skills Development***

The South African Skills Development Act (no 97 of 1998) has, according to the preamble of this act, the aim of providing "an institutional framework to devise and implement national, sector and workplace strategies to develop and improve the skills of the South African workforce; ...(and) to provide for learnerships that lead to recognized occupational qualifications..."

This means that the government is committed to the improvement of South African workers' skills by regulating the efforts of all interested parties to participate in training programs. This will certainly lead to higher levels of productivity and it is, therefore, in the interest of all businesses to lend their support to this program.

Many other countries have similar programs and employer ought to be aware of those and make use of them.

Technology in all sectors of industry and business is developing at a dizzying pace. Skills, which are relevant today, may be redundant in five years' time and training received a generation ago may be totally inappropriate for today's requirements. It is, therefore, in the interest of both employer and employee to become committed to ongoing training. If that does not happen productivity in will inevitably slide backwards and poverty will increase.

A system of performance appraisal, as set out in chapter 1, will help to identify the training needs of workers. Such a system will, in addition, evaluate the efficacy of any training program.

This does not necessary mean that workers should receive formal training to overcome certain weak points. In certain cases, this training may be profitable if a certain worker cannot be productive without a certain skill. Training should, actually, rather concentrate on the strengths of employees to help them to maximize their potential instead of trying to develop them in fields in which they are not interested or for which they are not suited. If their strengths are developed, they will become even better at those tasks for which they are already suited.

It is important to remember that the final responsibility for a worker's training and development rests ultimately with that worker himself or herself. He or she must have the necessary motivation and drive to develop, acquire new knowledge and learn new skills. Management can only create favorable circumstances and facilities for the training of employees. If these employees are not interested in their own development managers, mentors and supervisors can do little to alter this situation. If, however, the employees are committed to develop themselves, they will not be deterred by a lack of opportunities or facilities at the workplace since there are numerous alternative ways of achieving this.

Employers should, therefore, identify those workers who are motivated to receive ongoing training and help them along the road of further development and the unlocking of their potential.

The Skills Development Act has the object of motivating employers to provide more training to their staff to keep South Africa competitive on the world market and to ensure sustained economic growth.

This is a necessary measure, since South African companies spend on average only 3.3% of their total payroll on the training of personnel. This compares unfavorably with the USA and other major trading partners of South Africa who spend on average 5% and Japan that spends 10% of the payroll on training.

Anglo Platinum of Rustenburg, the world's largest platinum company, decided to budget R35-million-a year to improve the educational standards of its workforce. The ultimate aim was to empower black employees and women to reach certain goals of its

> *employment equity plan, including having 20% blacks in its top management by 2006. Training was provided for employees at all levels. The illiterate were taught to read and technical and managerial staff was given appropriate courses with the aid of the Wits Business School. An important spin-off of this investment was improved productivity on all levels.*

WORKING METHODS

A matter that is related to the skills needed to perform a certain job, although it must be distinguished from it, is the implementation of effective working methods.

Under effective working methods the following may by understood:

- Effective time management;
- Effective management and leadership practices (where applicable); and
- Effective management of work-related stress and burnout.

It is self-evident that both managers and employees ought to be taught effective working methods to increase their productivity.

- *Effective Time Management*

It is possible that certain workers may be very busy and work long hours but do not necessarily fill those hours with the correct tasks. If those workers constantly perform irrelevant work that has little relationship with the primary goals of their jobs, they simply are not effective.

To be effective, a worker does not necessarily have to work longer hours; that worker, though, must utilize the available time optimally. Some workers, however, have no control over their work pace:

- For instance, a worker who is supposed to receive an unfinished product from somebody else, to performs certain tasks on it and then to pass that product on to another worker, must adjust to the pace of the chain of workers.
- The work pace of a team is, likewise, dependent on the inputs of all the other members.

Many employees, on the other hand, have more discretion about the use of their time. One of the biggest sources of stress is time. When people feel that they have no control over the way they spend their time and when they must meet looming deadlines, they get stressed.

On the other hand, if one knows how to manage his time and utilizes his hours and minutes productively and effectively, he may keep his stress at bay. Good time management takes the following principles into consideration:

o Nobody can manage his or her time effectively without a proper diary – whether electronic or on paper. All the tasks that must be attended to on certain dates, such as appointments, meetings, and deadlines, must be listed in the diary to prevent them from being forgotten. If a task has been completed it can be crossed out. If appointments, meetings, and tasks have been captured in writing they need no longer be stored in the

person's memory – freeing his mind for more productive and creative tasks;
- See to it that lists of tasks awaiting completion are kept up-to-date (on paper or electronically in a diary or an annexure to the diary). Divide these lists into long term projects, medium term projects, short term tasks and tasks requiring only a few minutes to complete; these lists must be reviewed and renewed daily;
- The overall goal of the job or task has always to be kept in mind and the importance or urgency of all tasks is evaluated in the light of this goal. That determines the time allotted to each task;
- The overall goal of the job must be stipulated in the job description of that position; if a person does not know exactly what is expected of him or her and how his or her efforts dovetail into the activities and goals of the whole organization a lot of time may be wasted on unnecessary and unproductive actions;
- It is always good to plan a day or a week in advance and allot enough time for every task that must be completed to prevent unnecessary rushes;
- Urgent tasks with a deadline are completed first and the remaining time is utilized for less urgent tasks on the list of waiting tasks;
- Tasks for which a deadline is set should be started in good time; tasks that are rushed because of approaching deadlines are usually performed less efficiently while expensive and
- valuable time may be wasted by correcting mistakes later;
- Always strive for excellence rather than for perfection, since trying to attain perfection wastes valuable time (except in certain jobs where nothing but perfection is acceptable);

- It is always good to start the day with tasks that can be completed in less than two minutes, such as making a phone call, filing away a document or checking for e-mail – if a fairly large number of tasks can be completed in a relatively short time, then most tasks on the list for that day can be crossed out within an hour;

- When a period of a few minutes becomes available use it to complete a small task;
- Where possible, less important tasks are to be delegated to inferiors;
- It is important to learn to say 'no' to certain requests for help, especially when this will mean that certain other important tasks cannot be completed or when this help means performing tasks outside the job description for that particular position;
- Documents must, if possible, be handled only once. If a letter or memorandum is received it should immediately lead to a plan of action to give effect to its contents and thereafter it should be filed. If it is not possible to deal with it at once, post it to the "pending" tray and keep it for later action, together with other documents, which must lead to some sort of action;
- Divide incoming documents and messages in the "in" basket (letters, memoranda, e-mails, and voice mails) into the following categories: junk, reference and actionable. If something is classified as junk, throw it away. If something contains important information, file it in the appropriate file for

future reference. If something needs to be acted upon, try and deal with it immediately or keep it in the "pending" tray;
- Where possible, all tasks should be completed in one go; interruptions cause a waste of time since it takes time to pick up the threads after a delay;
- Chase away people who only want to chat;
- It isn't always possible to regulate interruptions such as incoming telephone calls or unexpected visits, but these should be handled in such a manner that the least possible time is lost;
- Avoid travelling as much as possible; rather use the telephone, the fax machine or e-mail to communicate with people elsewhere;
- If face-to-face meetings are essential, it is profitable to invite the other person to your office instead of travelling elsewhere;
- Record should be kept of all phone calls, interviews, conversations and meetings and these records should be kept in the appropriate files for future reference. Write down the date and time of the note because it may be important in future to know exactly when the relevant conversation or meeting took place; and
- Keep your working space tidy; throw out all pieces of junk, keep your files and books with reference material in one place, keep your files with correspondence in another place, arrange your equipment and utensils in such a manner as to minimize unnecessary movement and sort your supplies (paper, stamps, paper clips, staples, *etcetera*) into different categories and store them in drawers or trays. This will help you not to waste time while looking for a specific item.

In annexure A to this chapter a system of dealing with backlogs is explained.

> *An acquaintance of mine used to work in a team with several colleagues. One of the team members was always on the run. He was chronically late for appointments and meetings. Reports and assignments were only completed after expiry of the deadline. It seemed as if he never managed to catch up with the backlog on his desk. Although he was a talented man with good social skills and was well liked by everybody, there were understandably many complaints about his work. His trouble was bad time management. He could not cope with the stress of the job and eventually resigned.*

Bad time management

How long will you sleep, sluggard? When will you arise out of your sleep? A little sleep, a little slumber, a little folding of the hands to sleep: So your poverty will come as a robber, and your scarcity as an armed man (Prov 5: 9–11).

Time for work and for rest

Remember the Sabbath day, to keep it holy. You shall labor six days, and do all your work, but the seventh day is a Sabbath to YHWH your God. You shall not do any work in it, you, nor your son, nor your daughter, your man-servant, nor your maid-servant, nor your cattle, nor your stranger who is within your gates (Ex 20: 9–10).

- ***Effective Management and Leadership Practices***

Any employee who has supervisory functions over other workers has certain management and leadership functions. The supervision and leadership style of such people may either promote or undermine the goals of the organization and it is, therefore, necessary to help them to acquire a style that will benefit the organization.

The following functions may be expected from managers, supervisors, and leaders:

- Planning and decision-making;
- Organizing;
- Co-ordinating the efforts of others;
- Supervision and control;
- Advice to inferiors;
- Mentoring of novices;
- Budgeting and control over finances;
- Collecting and disseminating information;
- Managing the interpersonal relationships within the team or section;
- Representing the team or department within the context of the wider organization; and
- Communicating with the environment.

It is necessary that all managers, team leaders, and supervisors learn how to perform these functions effectively and efficiently – otherwise the productivity of their inferiors will inevitably suffer.

The way in which the above-mentioned tasks is performed is dependent on the leadership style of the person concerned. This style can, if necessary, be improved through training and counseling.

A good leadership style has the following characteristics:

o Good leaders have distinct goals and a vision of the future and they communicate these effectively to their followers;
o They inspire their followers to strive towards the realization of these goals by their example;
o Good leaders are attuned to the needs and welfare of their followers; they are tolerant, patient, just, fair, and considerate

and are not overly critical;
- Good leaders allow their followers to make mistakes and learn from them;
- A good leader is informed about the problems, needs, opportunities, and successes of his or her team;
- A good leader is available for the people under his/her care or supervision;
- A good leader is open for suggestions and ideas from those under him/her;
- Good leaders are experts on the matters under their control and know when quality work is being delivered;
- A good leader knows how to ask others to perform certain tasks without sounding like a dictator or a beggar;
- Good leaders demand solutions, not problems;
- A good leader represents the interests of his or her group towards the outside world; and
- A good leader shows confidence in his or her team or section and gives recognition for good work.

Where a person in a position of authority does not display these characteristics, it will be in the interest of the enterprise to develop his/her leadership qualities. A specialist from the personnel department or a competent consultant may be tasked to implement a program of leadership style training.

The theme of leadership will receive more attention in chapters 3 and 4.

> *A few people I have dealt with worked in a certain department of a large organization. The director of this department was very conscious of the fact that he was an important man with a grand title ('director') which emphasized this status and importance. He ruled his department in a very autocratic manner and tried to smother all initiative in those under him. Morale in this department deteriorated to such a degree that none of those I knew ten years ago still work there. One woman was prepared to sacrifice her pension and medical benefits just for the pleasure of resigning and telling this man in his face exactly what she thought of him.*

Leaders as servants

But Jesus called them to him, and said, "You know that the rulers of the Gentiles lord it over them, and their great ones exercise authority over them. It shall not be so among you, but whoever would become great among you will be your servant. Whoever would be first among you will be your bondservant" (Matt 20: 25–27).

- **Effective Management of Work-Related Stress and Burnout**

Any worker is prone to stress and burnout and this may influence productivity and work satisfaction negatively. Certain people are more prone to stress and burnout while others withstand it much better. There can be more than one reason for that.

It is important to remember that people do not react directly to stimuli from the external environment. They react rather to their subjective perceptions of those stimuli. What one person perceives as a threat another person may perceive as an opportunity or a challenge. One person may experience a situation as meaningless and overwhelming while another may experience it as meaningful or within his or her ability to handle.

When a certain situation is perceived as threatening, dangerous, overwhelming, and meaningless or out of control, it causes tension and eventually feelings of helplessness and despair. In other words, stress may cause distress – especially when that stress becomes excessive.

It was found in the USA that more than 80% of the adult population suffer from stress-related problems. The average employee takes 15 working days off per year for personal reasons and of those eleven days are used to handle stressful situations. The situation in South Africa may not be very different.

An investigation which the present writer undertook revealed that working conditions are the greatest source of stress in the lives of working people. The second most important source of stress is domestic problems.

The following aspects of a work situation may cause stress:

o A status which is not commensurate with the person's abilities and self-concept – which means either that such a person is appointed to a position for which he/she doesn't have the required training, aptitudes, or self-confidence or that that person has the perception that he/she has the necessary qualifications for a higher position while promotion is not forthcoming;
o Overloading of tasks and responsibilities – with the result that that person is always late with the completion of projects and tasks, is always rushed and always unsure of how to handle a given situation;
o Bad time management – the person does not know how to utilize available time effectively and is, therefore, always late, rushed and stressed;

- Role conflict and role overload – which means that somebody must fulfil conflicting roles or too many roles to handle comfortably;
- Lack of control over the situation – which means that the employee has little or no means of influencing the outcome of his/her efforts and that leads to frustration and feelings of powerlessness;
- When an employee is forced to perform tasks that run counter to his/her principles or interests;
- Repetitious and boring work – that is work that poses no challenge, is dull and does nothing to bolster a person's feelings of self-worth;
- Dangerous work – which means that the worker is always uncertain whether he/she won't be injured in some or other way and this uncertainty creates tension;
- Bad physical working conditions – e g noise, pollution, uncomfortable equipment, and furniture, over-crowded or cramped spaces and extreme temperatures, which may impair a worker's ability to perform optimally; and
- Responsibility for the welfare of others – which means that the burden of responsibilities may become too large to bear.

Apart from this, many factors from outside the work situation may increase the stress that a worker experiences. Marital problems, problems with children or other family members, housing problems, ill health, financial worries, and accidents may also contribute to the experience of stress by a worker.

In general, it may be said that stress is caused when a certain situation exists or is perceived to exist and it differs markedly from a preferred state of affairs. If an existing situation clashes with a person's interests, wishes, cultural background, or principles it is bound to cause resentment, unhappiness and stress.

If an employee is forced to work alongside other employees or under a supervisor with bad manners, unacceptable habits, and unethical practices, stress is the inevitable result.

An overdose of stress may cause many adverse reactions. Among these are –

- Decreased perceptual ability since senses and receptors are overloaded;
- Decreased ability to concentrate;
- Decreased ability to reach creative solutions for problems;
- Regression to infantile behavior;
- Destructive behavior such as aggression and alcohol abuse;
- An inability to handle relationships;
- Tiredness and an increased need for rest;
- Depression; and
- Reduced immunity from illness and various resulting ailments.

Burnout is the result of an overdose of stress. People whose work consists of the handling or care for other people, such as managers, teachers, social workers, nurses, priests, and police officers are especially prone to this syndrome. Somebody who experiences burnout may have all the above symptoms together with an emotional shut-down and a destruction of beliefs and value systems. This all mounts to a severe case of depression.

> *A couple turned to me for counselling. Although their marriage was a happy one, the man was depressed, slept badly, did not enjoy his life and work and quarreled with his wife. It turned out that he was the owner and manager of a small engineering firm and that his only daughter, who had helped him to run the business, was on the point of emigrating to Britain. He worked seven days a week, got no exercise and had no interests besides his work. After I prescribed a holiday, daily exercise and a better diet this man's depression lifted. When he learned to handle his stress more effectively, the symptoms of burn-out disappeared.*
>
> *Another client of mine, the managing director of a factory, had marital problems, problems with his hyperactive and demanding step-daughter and a running battle with his ex-wife over the supervision over their children. All this stress spilled over into his factory with the result that he was unable to deal effectively with conflict between him and certain staff members. To defuse this conflict and assist him to deal with his domestic problems he needed expert help.*

> *Elijah's depression and burn-out*
> Then Jezebel sent a messenger to Elijah, saying, "So let the gods do to me, and more also, if I don't make your life as the life of one of them by tomorrow about

> this time." When he saw that, he arose, and went for his life, and came to Beersheba, which belongs to Judah, and left his servant there. But he himself went a day's journey into the wilderness, and came and sat down under a juniper-tree: and he requested for himself that he might die, and said, "It is enough; now, oh, YHWH, take away my life; for I am not better than my fathers" (1 Kgs 19: 2–4).

It is clear that a stressed or burnt-out worker cannot perform as required. Employers may do much to lessen the effects of stress or to prevent the negative effects thereof. Help can be divided into two categories:

- Manipulation of the working environment to prevent unnecessary stress; and
- Teaching individuals to withstand stress more effectively.

The following may be done to *manipulate the environment:*

- Provide counseling facilities for stressed workers – either by employing a social worker or counselor to handle such cases or by referring stressed workers to an outside agency, such as the practice of a clinical or counseling psychologist;
- Restructure the person's job and give him/her the opportunity to learn something new and acquire new skills;
- Eliminate adverse working conditions by reducing noise, pollution, extreme temperatures, and cramped working quarters; and
- Provide social support systems.

People should be taught the following to *prevent stress and burnout:*

- A healthy life style with enough exercise, a nutritious diet and enough rest and relaxation;
- Effective time management;
- The building up of a social support system consisting of colleagues, friends, and family members;
- Increasing self-knowledge to accept personal limitations; and
- Adopting realistic goals to lessen disappointments and failures.

The personnel department and/or specialists from outside the organization may be utilized to implement an anti-stress program.

An enterprise that implements these strategies and programs will create more healthy and productive employees. Although it will surely cost something by way of money and manhours, the dividends will prove it to be a well-spent investment. Various surveys have shown that an employee assistance program is extremely profitable; for every dollar that is spent on counseling there is a saving of at least four dollars.

♦ ♦ ♦

From the preceding it must be clear that much can be done to help workers to change into more productive people. Although certain characteristics cannot be altered, it is necessary to consider these characteristics when expecting certain results from workers. Other characteristics, though, such as skills, knowledge and working methods can be changed through training and counselling.

Although certain characteristics of workers can be altered or developed to make them more productive it is not enough. If a worker is not motivated to perform optimally, he or she will remain unproductive. How motivation works is the subject of the next chapter.

Annexure A

How to Deal with Backlogs

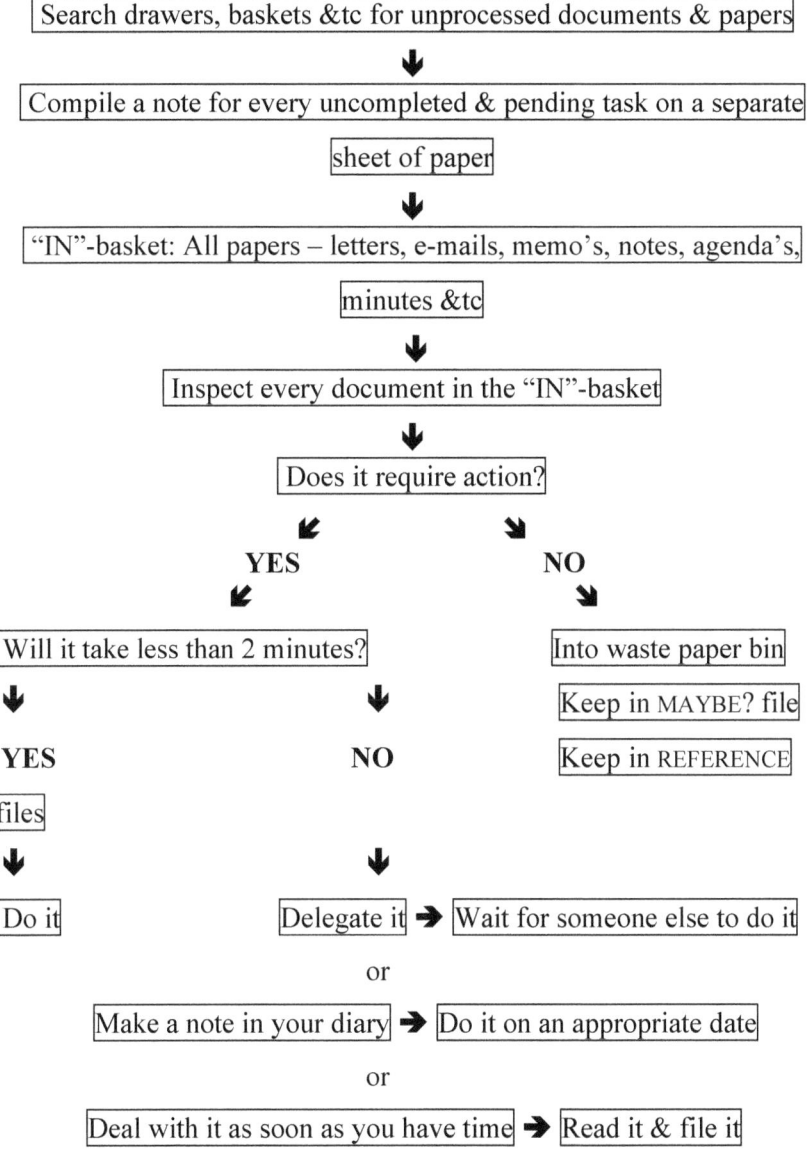

The Characteristics and Abilities of Workers and their Productivity

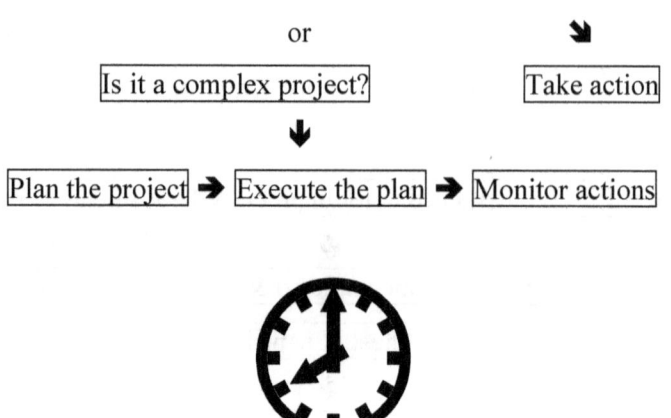

Chapter 4
The Motivation of Workers

Chapter outline:
- *Incentives and Intrinsic Motivation*
- *Providing in Biological, Psychological, and Spiritual Needs*
- *Inspiring Leadership*
- *Attitudes, Emotions, and Interests*
- *Values and Worldview*
- *Self-concept*
- *De-motivators*
- *Will Power*

INCENTIVES AND INTRINSIC MOTIVATION

When a crime is committed one of the first questions that everyone asks is, "What was the motive?"

Motives play a decisive role in human behavior. For every action (and every crime) there is some or other motive and that flows from the fact that human beings are free and responsible creatures who make choices and decisions and may be held accountable for their choices and decisions.

When we talk about boosting productivity the role of the motivation of workers cannot be left out of the picture. **Motivation** may be described as –

those factors that determine or regulate behavior. This implies that behavior is being caused by the person himself and that it is directed by determinants such as motives, needs, drives, and goals. Motivation is, therefore, to be distinguished from other determinants of behavior such as abilities and external stimuli from the environment.

Motivation stems from two sources: from within and from without. Psychologists distinguish between intrinsic motivation and extrinsic motivation.

Intrinsic motivation is essentially self-motivation. It flows from internal and subjective factors such as a person's attitude towards his or her work and life in general, his or her interests, value system, ideals, beliefs, feelings, self-confidence, self-concept, and willpower.

Extrinsic motivation is essentially the application of incentives and external determinants of behavior by an agency other than the person himself. Under these the following may be counted: the provision of ways and means for the fulfilment of biological, psychological, and spiritual needs, methods applied to coerce or force somebody into compliance, punishment, and rewards.

In the discussion that follows this distinction between intrinsic and extrinsic motivation will be maintained.

A distinction must also be made between extrinsic motivation and manipulation. Motivation boils down to getting people to do something because they want to do it or when they agree that it makes sense to do it. Manipulation, on the other hand, occurs where somebody in a powerful position gets people to do something because he or she wants them to do it. It is, therefore, clear that manipulation is not to be equated with motivation. Manipulation breeds resentment and that is bad for motivation and productivity.

The Motivation of Workers

Part of extrinsic motivation by an employer consists of the satisfaction of certain human needs:

PROVIDING IN PHYSICAL NEEDS

The most basic reason why people work is to provide in their biological needs. People need nourishment to stay alive and healthy, they need clothing to keep warm and they need housing to preserve their right to privacy and to protect them from the elements and other dangers. The salary a person receives as the fruits of his or her labors is used to satisfy these needs.

There is a perception that people can be enticed to work harder by promising to pay them more. This is a fallacy. It ought to be clear by this time that the boosting productivity rests on the interplay of many factors of which remuneration is only one. A pay rise may work up to a certain point to motivate a worker to work harder or better, but beyond that point other methods must be used.

Of course, nobody will be willing to work if there is no or too little monetary reward for his or her efforts. A worker's pay package is, after all, one of the more important items in his or her contract of service. When people have the perception that they are not rewarded adequately or fairly for their work, they are willing to try to remedy this situation, including strike action or seeking new jobs.

Every employer has the legal and moral obligation to pay

his employees. If an employer forsakes this duty dissatisfied workers have several options at their disposal to respond to this situation, such as going on strike or reporting the matter to the Department of Labor.

Of course, people do also work hard in voluntary organizations such as churches, welfare organizations, sports clubs, and service clubs without receiving any monetary rewards. This work is, usually, done in their free time and is something quite apart from their ordinary occupations. They do this partly because there are certain rewards in doing this voluntary work. These rewards are also applicable in occupational work and they must receive attention in the pages that follow.

PROVIDING IN PSYCHOLOGICAL NEEDS

Human beings are complex creatures with a wide variety of needs. Apart from their physiological needs, such as the needs for nourishment, water, oxygen, warmth, and rest, there are also psychological needs. Many of these needs are shared with higher animals.

Psychological needs may be classified under the following categories:

- The need for identity;
- The need for stimulation; and
- The need for security.

Research and experience have shown that people can be moved or motivated by providing in these psychological needs. It is, therefore, necessary to examine these needs in more detail to determine which role they play in motivation and productivity.

- **The Need for Identity**

Every person needs to be someone or somebody. He or she has the need to feel –

- recognized;
- important;
- respected;
- loved;
- wanted;
- needed by others;
- that he or she is a unique being;
- accepted as part of a family, a group of friends, a team of workers, or a community; and
- visible and heard.

The Preamble to the Universal Declaration of Human Rights proclaims that "recognition of the inherent dignity and of the equal and inalienable rights of all members of the human family is the foundation of freedom, justice and peace in the world." Article 1 of this Declaration affirms: "All human beings are born free and equal in dignity and rights."

It is, therefore clear that the concept of *human dignity* must always be kept in mind. Human dignity is closely tied to a person's identity.

Man Created in God's Image

God created man in his own image. In God's image he created him; male and female he created them. God blessed them. God said to them, "Be fruitful, and multiply, and replenish the earth, and subdue it. Have dominion over the fish of the sea, and over the birds of the sky, and over every living thing that moves on the earth" (Gen 1: 27–28).

A person's dignity and identity are linked to many attributes and characteristics. Some of the most important are the following:

- name;
- appearance;
- sex;
- age;
- family ties and heritage;
- personal history and achievements;
- membership of various groups, e g circle of friends, work team, profession, church or neighborhood;
- religious beliefs;
- nationality;
- cultural background;
- ties to a certain portion of the earth's surface, be it a country or a piece of real estate;
- interests and tastes;
- plans for the future; and
- self-concept.

All these attributes play a role in defining who and what that particular human being is. A person's identity is linked to his or her past and his or her identity has been formed by his or her life history. Some comments on the attributes listed above are necessary.

    A person's spoken name is the sound that he or she recognizes more easily than any other sound. Everybody likes hearing his or her name being spoken by somebody else. When somebody's name is mentioned in a crowded room, that person immediately picks up the sound of his or her name, even if many other voices speak at the same time.

A person's appearance is important to him or her and everybody likes to look good.

An older person likes to be recognized as a younger person's senior and to be respected as somebody with more experience and wisdom.

People talk easily about their experiences and their achievements since that gives them a certain importance. A person's identity has to do with the people with whom he or she associates since human beings are social creatures; therefore, all of us belong to a number of formal and informal groups. The most important group to which a person belongs is usually his or her family; a family's honor and reputation will therefore be defended vehemently.

Religious beliefs and affiliations help people to discover and strengthen their identity when they are assured of the fact that they are God's children and that they are part of a body of people accepting the same beliefs and principles as they do.

Everybody dislikes being a nobody, a nonentity, a non-person, a cog in a giant machine, a number in a gigantic system, or a faceless member of "the public" or "the workforce". Everybody has the need to feel loved, recognized and to feel good about himself or herself. Some people will go to great lengths to draw attention to themselves. Other people will rather die than appear different from the group to which they belong, since that will jeopardize their acceptance into the group and, therefore, their sense of identity.

When this need for identity is not satisfied people easily feel useless, superfluous and without direction or a goal in life.

When a worker's need for recognition is not satisfied in the work situation, he or she will have little motivation to do more than the absolute minimum. It is therefore imperative that one goes

The Motivation of Workers

to great lengths to satisfy this need in every member of the staff. There are various ways in which this can be done.

When a concern or organization has a certain status in the world employees like to be associated and identified with it. They like to be known as people who work for and belong to firm A, supermarket B, factory C, or company D. Employers should not take this loyalty for granted but they should foster it. It is, after all, part of the psychological contract between employer and employee.

Many concerns try to strengthen this loyalty and identity by issuing their members with nametags, uniforms, or other identifying items such as handbags, ties, pens or crockery with the company's logo or name printed prominently on each item. Apart from the fact that these identifying items serve as advertisement for the concern in question they also bolster the employees' need for identity.

Since membership of a group forms part of a person's identity many concerns have organized their workforce into permanent teams of not more than ten or eleven members. Being part of such a team strengthens the individual's sense of identity. This leads to a sense of loyalty towards the other team members and the team as a whole. A good team leader should take advantage of this loyalty and identification with the team to strengthen the workers' motivation not to let the team down by performing poorly. It makes sense, therefore, to conduct team building exercises.

An important way of giving recognition to employees is to award special rewards for exceptional service and to publicize this fact. For this reason, many concerns have their own internal news letters or staff magazines where this type of recognition can be published. Special awards can take on many forms, such as certificates, plaques, medals, watches, lunch with the boss, bonuses, shopping vouchers, extra days leave, rises in salary or promotion.

The giving of recognition should, however, not be confined to such special efforts. Giving recognition and satisfying workers' need for identity should be an ongoing activity. Good managers, supervisors and leaders have the knack of letting all their inferiors or followers feel special and appreciated. They give praise and thanks for good work, respect everybody's individuality, uniqueness, and human dignity and take everybody seriously. Nobody is ever humiliated – even if that person is guilty of misconduct, negligence, or poor work performance and has to be punished or reprimanded.

In order to be able to give this recognition it is advisable that the manager or supervisor knows exactly what is going on in the concern or in his or her department. This information doesn't necessarily feature in official reports and therefore it will be necessary to tune in on the informal grapevine of the organization and communicate directly with people far below on the chain of command.

Certain concerns have the habit of attaching very important-sounding titles to very ordinary jobs to motivate the job incumbents. The best example I have come across is the title of "garbage disposal executive" for an ordinary dustman. If this practice is not accompanied by respect for the person, real responsibility, and regard for his or her contributions, this strategy doesn't work. Organizations with an impressive collection of titles very often are unhealthy organizations with a top-heavy management structure.

> *It is told of Alexander the Great that he shared all the hardships of his soldiers when they went on campaigns to conquer the world. After every battle he would move amongst his men and hear from them their stories about the dangers they faced. Napoleon is reputed to have known the name of every officer in his army as well as the regiment to whom each one belonged. This recognition of the identity of their followers made Alexander and Napoleon such great leaders. They managed to motivate their men to follow them to the ends of the earth.*
>
> *A man I knew well committed suicide and afterwards his widow and I had several counselling sessions. He was a plant manager in a large industrial concern, but he lost his job when the board of directors decided to downsize and to retrench all employees above the age of 55. Although he was awarded a handsome severance package and a generous pension, he suddenly became a nobody. According to his widow, the loss of his identity as manager of a division was too much to bear and he, therefore, became so depressed that he shot himself.*

> *Praise for a good servant*
> His lord said to him, "Well done, good and faithful servant. You have been faithful over a few things, I will set you over many things. Enter into the joy of your lord" (Matt 25: 21).'

- ### *The Need for Stimulation*

Nobody likes boredom. The human brain is wired and programmed in such a way as to seek continuous stimulation. When a situation arises where no stimulation is received the brain creates its own stimulation.

People who, as part of an experiment, have been isolated in soundproof and dark cells or in tanks with lukewarm water with a breathing apparatus started to hallucinate after some time. They saw, heard, tasted, felt, and smelled non-existent things and events. Where their external circumstances provided the minimum amount of stimulation their brains started to create their own sights, sounds, tastes, sensations, and smells.

This need for stimulation is already present in babies and small children. They have the constant urge to explore their own bodies and the world around them. They try out various forms of behavior to test the reactions of the people who care for them. Infants who are not regularly handled, fondled, and stroked easily develop various ailments and psychological problems.

There is a vast industry to satisfy the need for stimulation. People spend large sums of money on entertainment in its various forms. They pay to see films, plays, music concerts, musicals, television programs, or sporting events. They spend money to dance, to gamble, to go on holiday, or to travel. All this entertainment and stimulation isn't necessary to sustain life but people still seem to need it. Nobody likes boredom and, therefore, the need for stimulation is focused on the present.

Religion and church membership seem to provide in people's need for stimulation. Church services are meant to be inspiring, uplifting, and rousing. People are challenged to change their lives and try out new life styles. Singing and chanting with a group of people is a usually a pleasant experience. Religion provides people with certain goals in their lives and that is an antidote to boredom.

Elderly people who are confined to their beds or wheel chairs and are deaf or blind easily die of boredom. Apart from the fact that their need for identity isn't satisfied they also have a deficit of stimulation since they have very little opportunity to

The Motivation of Workers

communicate and interact with other people or to experience anything interesting.

If workers don't find adequate stimulation in their work situation their motivation to perform adequately easily disappears. It is, nevertheless, true that many workers are satisfied with repetitive and boring tasks and that they gladly continue to work in those circumstances. Apart from the fact that they need the money such jobs usually have other spin-offs. In many cases they perform the repetitive movements mechanically while their attention is elsewhere – with the radio or the television that is playing or with the conversations they are conducting with fellow workers.

A few decades ago, the concept of *job enrichment* appeared. That was an endeavor to try and make jobs more interesting and thereby to motivate employees to do more.

Many industries nowadays are organized differently from those of a generation ago. Computers and machines are performing many repetitive and routine tasks while the human operators can give attention to more interesting and creative tasks. Jobs can be made more stimulating and interesting by giving the person concerned attainable goals to strive for, as well as more responsibility and discretion to make decisions. Where a job is structured in such a manner as to call for creative solutions to problems there is no place for boredom.

When people get information on where their efforts fit into the wider and bigger picture and where their part of the work is crucial for the success of the whole it will do much to satisfy their need for identity and their need for stimulation.

An alarmingly large number of young people nowadays experiment with drugs such as cannabis, ecstasy, and methamphetamine. Many adults find this very worrying and puzzling. What is more

> *puzzling, is the fact that a large percentage of these young people stop taking these drugs after some time. The explanation isn't hard to find. Adolescents try these drugs since many of their friends use them and because it gives them the 'kicks'. In other words, experimenting with drugs fulfil their needs for identity and stimulation.*

- ### The Need for Security

It is important for human beings to feel safe and secure. They have the need to know what to expect from the future. Although people sometimes do dangerous things in their quest for stimulation, such as bungy jumping or motor cycle racing, they also need to know that their circumstances and future prospects are relatively secure. One important reason why people work is to satisfy this need for financial security.

Human beings want to know where they stand in relation to other significant people in their lives. That is why it is important for family members and spouses to continuously reassure each other of their love and affection.

One of the reasons why religion plays such an important role in people's lives is the fact that they constantly need to be reminded and assured of God's loving care and of the fact that their lives have not been in vain.

The insurance industry plays an important role in the satisfaction of the need for security. People invest in insurance policies, medical aid schemes, pension schemes, and funeral schemes to alleviate their worries about the future and possible mishaps.

In previous decades people had more job security than nowadays. Although the labor legislation of many countries makes it difficult for employers to dismiss workers for whatever reason, the fact is that many enterprises do dismiss workers for operational reasons. Other workers are employed on a temporary basis or are treated as consultants or independent contractors whose contracts may or may not be renewed after expiry. This is the result of the fact that the continued operation of many enterprises in today's volatile global market is uncertain. Technology develops at such a horrific pace that many jobs that are in demand today may become redundant in a few years' time.

It is, therefore, not always possible for management to do much about the job security of the workforce. It is just not possible to guarantee continued employment for the next ten or twenty years.

What management can do is to be totally honest with workers and their trade unions. No false promises should be made, information regarding the financial position and future prospects of the company should be divulged and the promise should be given that all dismissals due to redundancy or retrenchments will be handled in accordance with legal prescriptions.

Another way in which workers' need for security should be met is when management is absolutely fair in enforcing discipline in accordance with the rules of the company. Employees should know these rules and know exactly what is expected of them. They should also know what the penalties for certain infringements are. When there is no consistency in the way workers are treated or disciplinary matters are handled the result is uncertainty about the outcomes of certain behaviors. This uncertainty is certainly not conducive to good labor relations and to optimum productivity.

Although managers and supervisors are not supposed to be policemen, they cannot tolerate poor discipline, unethical and illegal acts, and behavior that impacts negatively on the well-being of the organization. Dishonesty, theft, absenteeism, aggressive behavior towards co-workers, supervisors or clients, insubordination, sabotage, and destruction of property cannot be tolerated and should be punished – even with dismissal in serious cases. Where applicable, infringements of the law should be reported to the Police.

PROVIDING IN SPIRITUAL NEEDS

When *spiritual* needs are mentioned, we do not necessarily mean needs on the religious plane. *Spiritual needs* are wider than religious needs, although they include them. The meaning of the word *spiritual*, as it is used here, relates to the *spirit* of man, to the highest human functions, which distinguish man from the animal world.

Under *spiritual needs* we understand the need of every person –

- to make sense out of events and to grasp the meaning of life;
- to be free to decide how the future will be faced; and
- to be recognized as a responsible being.

o *The Meaning of Life*

People who cannot find meaning in life, whether it be in a religious or philosophical sense, live in an existential vacuum. When life appears to be meaningless there is nothing to live or exist for and then people simply vegetate.

Such a state of affairs may exist where people have lost everything, including their human dignity. That happened, for instance, in the Nazi extermination camps during the Second World War or the Communist labor camps in Siberia for dissidents. The Austrian psychiatrist, Viktor Frankl, became world famous because of his experiences in such a Nazi death camp where he could inspire his fellow inmates to continue experiencing meaning in their sufferings and therefore to endure all their privations. It was his experience that people who had given up hope of survival and for whom their suffering made no sense died easily, while those who retained their hope and continued to find meaning in life survived more readily.

Frankl concluded that people would be able to endure almost anything if it makes sense to them and life has not lost its meaning. This need for meaning is, therefore, according to him, the deepest need any person can ever have.

When people experience life as meaningless the temptation to engage in dangerous and self-destructing activities, such as crime, alcohol or drug abuse, or unsafe sex, becomes overpowering. Somebody who does not have anything to live for will do anything just for excitement or pleasure – even if he or she may end up in prison or may contract a fatal disease. "What does it matter, anyway?" they argue, "life has no meaning and, therefore, no value. You may just as well do what you like and enjoy it."

This nihilistic and hedonistic approach to life usually occurs in affluent societies where children are allowed everything and receive anything they desire. There is no incentive to work hard since Dad and Mom will always provide the cash. To drive away the boredom and meaningless of life these juveniles easily revert to anti-social, criminal, or self-destructing behavior.

Many of the hippies of the sixties and seventies and New Age travelers of latter years come from such nihilistic backgrounds. To find meaning in life they either became rebels against the establishment or they turn to some or other exotic religion or philosophy.

Religion and philosophy play a crucial role in helping

people to find meaning in life. The teachings of the Bible or of a religious leader may assist people to discover their place in the universe, a goal in life or a vocation. Religious people experience life as meaningful since they are assured of God's love and they are convinced that God has a purpose with their lives.

> *God's purpose*
> We know that all things work together for good for those who love God, to those who are called according to his purpose(Rom 8: 28).

It is clear that nihilists, people who cannot find meaning in life and to whom all events make no sense or people whose need for meaning in life has been frustrated, cannot be productive workers. They do not see the need to work, to improve their skills, to contribute to the well-being of others or to contribute to society.

Since nihilists are not interested in work and seldom apply for jobs they won't be much of a problem for the management of any organization. There is little need to weed them out from the job applicants before appointments are made.

Management should, however, beware not to *create* nihilists in their existing workforce.

Where people have a deep-felt need to discover meaning in life – and in their work – it should be profitable that management create circumstances in which employees find meaning in their work. Meaning is something that must be discovered and no two people attach the same meaning to experiences and events.

Management may help employees to see the bigger picture and discover meaning in their work. Employees must be assisted to see that their efforts amount to more than only increasing the profits of the organization. If management has the vision that their organization offers products or services that positively benefit mankind then this enthusiasm and drive can be communicated to all employees.

Motivation is always goal-orientated. When people are motivated, they are motivated to move in a certain direction to achieve some or other goal. Management should, therefore, have a clear vision of the future and the methods to reach these future goals. All the members of the organization ought to know what this vision and these goals entail and they must see it as something worthwhile to work for and strive towards.

Every employee should know where his or her work fits into the whole and which contribution he or she makes to realize the goals and dreams of the organization. Employees should be aware of what the organization stands for and how it is supposed to benefit mankind – and be able to explain this to outsiders.

Business concerns exist to make a profit. There is nothing wrong with this motive for being in business. But when profit-making is the only reason why an organization exists then that organization is doomed to become extinct. Then the organization and its members are bound to become nihilists, hedonists, or gross materialists for whom life and labor ultimately have no meaning. But when a concern also exists to render some or other positive service to society or to improve the quality of life of its customers and clients (and society in general) then that concern and its workers have a worthwhile goal and vision. In such circumstances it is easier to motivate and to inspire the workforce to participate in this worthy venture.

> *I have counselled quite a number of people who had lost a loved one – a spouse, a parent, a sibling, or a child. One of the aspects of these tragedies that was particularly difficult to bear, was the fact that these deaths seemed so meaningless. In some cases, the deceased had a long and painful suffering before dying eventually.*
>
> *In other cases, the departed ones were still young people with a bright future ahead of them. In all these cases, they were people who were loved. This agony over the seemingly senselessness of their deaths made grieving a very difficult and painful experience. When the grieving family members eventually came round to see their losses as opportunities to grow personally, to gain better self-knowledge, to become better members of society and to gain more insight in the plights of other suffering people, then these losses started to make sense and the pain of their grieving became easier to tolerate.*

- **The Need for Freedom and the Need for Responsibility**

Another fundamental spiritual need of human beings is their need to be free and to exercise this freedom in responsibility.

Freedom cannot exist without responsibility. These two are inseparable just as the two sides of a coin cannot be separated from each other.

Freedom is about choices and decisions. An unfree person doesn't have the capacity or liberty to make choices or decisions, but a free person may choose between alternatives and decide on a certain course of action. When anybody makes a choice or decision several questions must be answered. It must be asked whether the choice will be profitable or harmful, whether it is a good or a bad choice, whether it will affect other people adversely or profitably and whether that choice can be defended on ethical grounds as being the right choice.

Our choices and decisions affect other people and, therefore, we must take good moral and ethical principles into consideration. We are ultimately responsible to ourselves, our parents, our family, our workplace, our society, mankind in general, and to God. We receive our ethical commandments, our morality and our laws from these agencies and they demand that we make the right decisions and good choices about the direction of our lives and our behavior.

Responsibility

So then each one of us will give account of himself to God (Rom 14: 12).

But let each man test his own work, and then he will take pride in himself and not in his neighbor. For each man will bear his own burden (Gal 6: 4–5).

Normal, well-adjusted workers have the need to perform their work in relative freedom and responsibility. This gives them scope to delve into their creativity, to make their own decisions and to feel important. When they are given a certain amount of decision-making power and responsibility their need for identity will be largely satisfied.

Where workers are denied any freedom and responsibility they will start to behave as irresponsible people. Because their psychological and spiritual needs are being thwarted their motivation and loyalty towards the organization will be low.

They will not be motivated to prevent losses and may even turn into active saboteurs by rendering the minimum amount of work. Where workers' need for freedom and responsibility is being satisfied and they get the message that they are trusted, that will entice them to behave as responsible people. They will feel responsible for the welfare of the organization with which they identify themselves and therefore they will help to prevent losses and to work towards the goals of the organization.

Many organizations organize their workers into teams or tasks forces consisting of several members. These teams or task forces are given a large measure of autonomy to manage themselves and to decide how they will complete the project assigned to them.

It has been found that the productivity of such a relatively independent team is higher than that of individuals working in large groups or in groups that are tightly supervised. This is because the team members' need for freedom and responsibility is being satisfied.

INSPIRING LEADERSHIP

The topic of leadership has already been raised in the previous chapter. A few more thoughts must be added.

- *Managers and leaders*

Not every manager is a good leader, although it is desirable that he or she be both. Good managers have control over their budgets, perform enough planning, have clear goals and know how to reach those goals. Usually, they drive or force their inferiors to reach these goals. But that is not to say that they also are leaders of people. To be a really good manager one also must know how to get people to follow you.

Leadership may be described as –

> *the interpersonal influence that occurs when one person is able to gain voluntary compliance from another in the direction of certain desired goals.*

A leader must fulfil the following functions:

- He or she gives guidance and direction;
- He or she energizes, mobilizes, and motivates people;
- He or she help people to participate in his or her vision and to rise to challenges; and
- He or she helps people to rise above adverse circumstances and dark times.

- *Qualities of Inspiring Leaders*

People will follow a leader if hat leader has legitimacy in their eyes, which legitimacy depends on several factors. The leader must have authority, but he or she must also have integrity, knows what the problems and needs of his or her followers are, shows a good example, and have the ability to inspire his or her followers.

Sometimes a distinction is made between task-oriented leaders and people-oriented leaders, although somebody can be both at the same time. Both styles have a place.

A leader who is low on both task-orientation and people-orientation is an ineffective and confused leader.

The leader who is low on task-orientation and high on people-orientation isn't really a leader, but rather a social worker.

The leader who scores high on task-orientation and low on people-orientation is usually also a bad leader. He or she may be described as a small dictator. In certain circumstances, such as an emergency, is necessary to be highly task-orientated. Then there isn't time to take people's feelings into consideration or hear everybody's concerns or opinions. Then certain tasks must performed in a minimum of time and all that matters is the end-result.

In normal circumstances, when everything is running more or less smoothly, a good leader will be task-orientated, as well as people-orientated. The good leader will be attuned to how people feel, think, and act. Their concerns will be his or her concerns and he or she will be sensitive to their needs. In other words: a good leader will know how to motivate his or her followers by providing in their biological, psychological, and spiritual needs. But the good leader also knows that his followers must achieve certain goals and that tasks have to be assigned to reach those goals. That means that order and discipline will have to be maintained

But more than that is expected of any good leader. To really motivate people, it is necessary that the leader *inspire* his or her followers. When people are inspired, they are willing to go to great lengths to achieve some or other goal.

To be inspiring, a leader must have integrity and show a good example. A leader who expects other people to be honest, hard-working, considerate, and conscientious but doesn't himself or herself live up to those standards certainly won't achieve the desired results. People will rather follow his or her bad example than his or her orders and directives. This is bad for productivity.

In other words: a manager or supervisor who is dishonest, comes late for work, tells lies, cheats and disregards company rules and the law will never be able to motivate his or her inferiors to be honest, punctual, truthful, reliable, and respectful of rules and laws.

To be inspiring a leader must himself or herself be inspired and motivated. When a leader has a clear vision of what he or she has to accomplish, shows enthusiasm for his or her work, demonstrates a passion for doing things right and efficiently and when he or she communicates the message that he or she is only satisfied with the highest standards in his or her own work, then all the followers will be carried along. This inspiration and enthusiasm will prove to be contagious. Then the leader will have followers instead of only inferiors.

The reverse is also true. When a leader is unmotivated, lazy, and lethargic that example will also prove to be contagious.

This principle may also be investigated from another angle. There are basically three ways of controlling peoples' actions: might, authority, or influence.

A leader exercises *might* when he or she is in a powerful position to reward or punish people, to give them pleasure or pain. A leader utilizes *authority* by relying on a position or a rank in a hierarchy to compel people to perform certain actions. During the industrial revolution and till the first few decades of the twentieth century the exercise of might and authority was the method of choice for managers in business or industry.

Nowadays it is realized that workers can only be influenced to do their best when managers and leaders rely on *influence* based on personal qualities and competence. When a leader has a personal and moral influence over his or her followers, they will willingly do his or her bidding.

The good leader is also somebody who realizes that the motivation of followers is an ongoing process. People who are motivated today won't necessarily be motivated tomorrow. Any program to raise motivation must, therefore, be a continuous process that must be updated and adapted regularly. The leader will, therefore, hold regular introspection to ascertain whether his or her own motivation is still strong enough to influence and inspire others.

The bottom line is that a manager or supervisor will not be able to motivate other people if he or she isn't highly motivated himself or herself.

When a leader really leads by his or her example then it isn't necessary to bribe, cajole, beg, coerce, or force people to do a good job. A good leader manages to create followers who follow him or her willingly and are prepared to exert themselves to please the leader.

ATTITUDES, EMOTIONS, AND INTERESTS

It has been demonstrated countless times that a worker who has a negative attitude or negative feelings towards work and shows little interest in his or her work will never be a productive worker. It is, therefore, important that managers and supervisors know how attitudes, feelings and interests influence work behavior and how they can be changed.

Attitudes may be defined as –

complexes of emotions (feelings) and beliefs that people have regarding specific ideas, situations, objects, people, or groups of people and which may become visible in certain behaviors.

Attitudes, then, are mixtures of feelings and thoughts; they operate on both the emotional and the cognitive levels and are, therefore, difficult to change.

> *When I was a part-time chaplain the South African Army during the eighties of the previous century, I regularly encountered national servicemen or conscripts who hated the Army and showed their feelings by being sulky and doing the absolute minimum to stay out of trouble. I also met battalion and company commanders, usually professional soldiers, who had good people skills, showed an active interest in the well-being of their troops and who managed to instill a culture of camaraderie and loyalty in their units, which led to good discipline, also during battle situations when every man had to do his duty automatically.*
>
>

Attitudes are usually fairly stable and are the result of a history of encounters or experiences a person has had with the idea, situation, object, person, or group in question. The longer this history, the more enduring the attitudes usually are. An attitude may rest on accurate or inaccurate perceptions, as well as certain biases, and may therefore be appropriate or inappropriate.

A hypothetical example may illustrate this: A new worker joins a team and hears negative rumors regarding the managing director of the firm. He hears that this person is haughty and unfriendly. In reality, the managing director is shy and has few social skills. The aversion the new worker feels towards the MD is, therefore, not appropriate and may change when he comes to know the MD better.

Interests are related to attitudes, although they are not identical. When someone is interested in something it means that that something is somehow important to him or her. This interest is also the result of a person's history, but it may also be related to that person's capabilities and aptitudes.

When a child finds that he is good at hitting a ball with a bat or a racquet he is likely to become interested in cricket, baseball, or tennis. When he finds, on the other hand, that he always misses the ball and that he has no aptitude or ability to perform the correct movements, his interest in these sports will surely never develop.

It is necessary that workers have positive attitudes towards work in general, their jobs and their workplace and that they be interested in their work.

Employers tend to hire workers with enthusiasm, a positive attitude towards work and with an interest in the tasks they must perform. It would be looking for trouble to appoint persons with little interest or a wrong attitude since their motivation will be very low. It is possible to measure people's attitudes and interests by means of certain psychometric instruments. Interviews may also reveal something in this regard, although job applicants may deliberately represent themselves in a more positive light to get the job.

The bottom line is that the best strategy to motivate a workforce is to appoint people who are already motivated.

When attitudes among the workforce are not conducive to productivity they may be changed, although this by no means always easy. Attitudes may be changed in the light of new experiences, new information or when a person's interests shift. When you help people to have pleasant feelings or emotions about something their attitudes may be altered.

VALUES AND WORLDVIEW

- *Values and Beliefs as Motivators*

Every person has certain beliefs regarding the world, life in general, his fellow human beings, and his work. These beliefs are the result of that person's upbringing, culture, and life history. Such beliefs are related to that person's religious views and/or philosophy of life. Many of these ideas may be patently wrong, irrational, untrue, or bad but since they are part of that person's life history it isn't easy to convince somebody that those beliefs must be changed. Those beliefs usually have an emotional undercurrent and when somebody's beliefs are being challenged an emotional reaction sets in which prevents any clear-headed appraisal of any new ideas.

A significant part of these beliefs has to do with that person's convictions regarding right or wrong or good and bad; in other words, with that person's values, ethical standards, and morals. These values and morals guide that person's actions and behavior and they are, therefore, important motivators.

The human conscience guides men's actions
When Gentiles who don't have the law do by nature the things of the law, these, not having the law, are a law to themselves, in that they show the work of the law written in their hearts, their conscience testifying with them, and their thoughts among themselves accusing or else excusing them (Rom 2: 14–15).

Every person continuously makes choices about some or other course of action. At a subconscious level he or she asks himself or herself whether a certain action will be advantageous or disadvantageous, good or bad, acceptable or unacceptable. These choices are made against the background of the values and beliefs that are dear to that person. If somebody believes that it is wrong to tell lies that belief will prevent him or her from distorting the truth. If a person believes that it is praiseworthy to help elderly people then one can expect that person to act accordingly.

It is self-evident that a worker's values, worldview, religious beliefs, and philosophy of life will also impact decisively on his or her work behavior and motivation in the workplace.

- If a worker, for instance, does not regard it as wrong to steal from his or her employer then theft will inevitably occur.
- If another worker has no ambition to be promoted to a higher position, then his or her performance will surely not be of a particularly high standard.
- If certain employees regard all employers as oppressors, it is to be expected that they will make life as difficult as possible for their employers.

- **The Challenge in South Africa**

It is my belief that the greatest impediment to greater productivity in South Africa lies in this field. It is my, and many other observers', conclusion that a large percentage of South African workers just are not interested in their work or in achievements of any sort and that their work motivation, therefore, is at rock bottom. The World Competitiveness Yearbook found that one of the main reasons why the productivity of South African workers is relatively low has to do with the values of the population. To put it bluntly: there just is not a culture of honest hard work and productivity in this country.

This explains why so many local authorities and government departments are dysfunctional and why corruption has become endemic in the public service.

This state of affairs is to a certain extent a legacy of the past. Members of previously disenfranchised groups had little opportunity of progressing in their work and participating in the decision-making process regarding politics, industry, and business. That killed any interest in work they might have had. After the democratization of South Africa in 1994 they got the opportunity to participate fully in politics, the industrial world, and business, and there is surely no lack of motivation to achieve a certain status and to receive the rewards that go with such a status. There is, however, no great loyalty or emotional commitment to these institutions since most of them have been created by the former "oppressors". In other words, these people are not (yet) prepared to fulfil their part of the bargain under the psychological contract between employer and employee.

Another reason for this situation may be a deep-rooted feeling of inadequacy and worthlessness in many people from formerly disadvantaged groups that suffered serious discrimination due to their skin color. They simply do not believe that they are able to achieve something worthwhile in life and, therefore, they do not even attempt to accomplish anything.

A culture of demands has taken root in South Africa. In the previous dispensation the government and the white minority were seen as the oppressors and the oppressed demanded to be given what they perceived to be their rights. In the long run that strategy worked. Many of these demands were eventually conceded. Many people still demand from government to supply everything they need and wish without seeing the necessity to work for whatever they desire.

A few generations ago, a subsistence agricultural system prevailed in the black communities. Nobody thought of planting surplus crops and only enough was produced to provide in immediate needs. Work in the fields was regarded as women's work while men were supposed to tend the animals. This system obviously cannot work in the twenty-first century with a much denser population and an economy that must compete with the rest of the globe. The old mindset is, however, still prevalent to a certain extent and people still do not see the need for higher productivity.

This mindset is still visible where certain people do not regard it as necessary to work since one or more family members do have jobs. They regard it as the duty of those who have employment to support the rest of the family. This way of thinking places high value on family ties – which is to be admired – but it doesn't lead to a workforce which is motivated to perform optimally and to the eradication of poverty.

This situation is certainly to be found in many other countries where the productivity of the workforce is low.

The greatest challenge to higher productivity in South Africa, therefore, lies in the field of values and worldviews. It isn't easy to change beliefs and convictions which have been held since childhood and which have deep emotional roots. This isn't impossible, though. There are programs and courses which almost approach brain-washing and where employees can be motivated to become high achievers. This task must be given to skilled psychologists and educational experts to achieve the desired results.

This is a very demanding task since the people whose values and mindsets have to be changed are people who have the right of freedom of thought and the right to have their human dignity respected. These psychologists and educators must tread warily and carefully where these issues are concerned.

Although the thought of something akin to brain-washing may sound unacceptable to some people it is highly necessary that South Africa's workers become more achievement-orientated and that their values reflect the needs and challenges of our times. Nobody cannot afford to have workers who are not motivated. If the goal of helping workers to acquire more appropriate values and insights is not reached the war against poverty and misery will almost definitely not be won.

A campaign to instill new values and ideas must not be restricted to workers. All segments of the population must somehow be reached. The sooner this can be done the better and therefore a program to motivate school children must be regarded as a high priority.

SELF-CONCEPT

Every person has a self-concept. Everyone has certain ideas about who and what he or she is, what his or her capabilities are, what he or she is supposed to become, what his or her weak points are, and what other people think or ought to think about him or her. Everyone has certain convictions about the person he or she can become and ought to become.

If a worker is convinced that he or she isn't capable of performing a certain task then he or she won't even try to do it.

There will, in other words, be no motivation to try anything. If a supervisor can, however, convince a worker that he or she, after all, does have the capacity to succeed in that task, that person may try. If he or she succeeds then his or her self-concept must be adjusted. What was regarded as impossible becomes possible and motivation will inevitably soar.

> *Before Roger Bannister broke the 4-minute barrier in the mile on 6 May 1954 no one believed that it was possible to run this distance in less than 4 minutes. The previous record of a few seconds more than 4 minutes stood for many years. Shortly after he broke this record many athletes succeeded in repeating this performance – simply because they came to believe this to be possible and within their abilities. Bannister smashed a psychological barrier.*

An important part of any training program in the workplace must be an endeavor to convince workers that they are able to reach certain achievements. Their self-concepts must be expanded and they ought to be made to believe in themselves. It will be worthwhile to set them before certain challenges, inter alia by organizing competitions between individuals, teams, and departments.

People perform according to their self-concepts. If somebody's performance is on par with his or her self-concept, he or she will feel comfortable. If people over-perform or under-perform, they will feel uncomfortable and the result is that they will adjust their performance to suit their self-concept. It follows that it will pay to improve workers' self-concept. This can be done by treating them with respect, acknowledging the fact that they are competent, mature, and responsible adults. Rewards and recognition for good work and training programs to improve workers' skills and knowledge will also result in improved self-concepts.

In the past, many under-privileged South Africans had very low self-concepts. They never thought that they had the ability to become artisans, mechanics, book-keepers, managers, doctors, engineers, judges, or scientists.

This theory ought to be put into practice. People must start believing that they are equals and act accordingly. They must be assisted to believe in themselves and to become better motivated workers.

DE-MOTIVATORS

There are many things managers can do to motivate the workforce which have been discussed in the previous sections of this chapter. There are, however, certain things they must refrain from doing in order not to undermine the motivation of their workers. The following list is certainly not exhaustive but it will give a good idea of which de-motivators must be eliminated or avoided.

- o Do not treat your workers with disrespect. If you trample upon their self-esteem and human dignity you cannot expect of them to respect you or be motivated to do their best. When you show them respect, even to those who are on the bottom level of the organization, then you can expect to receive their respect in return. And when they respect you, they will be more willing to accept your leadership.
- o Do not treat employees as mere production units or labor units and ignore their humanity. This attitude will certainly undermine or destroy their motivation and loyalty towards the organization. Their full potential will never be unlocked and

The Motivation of Workers

their unique bodily, psychological, and spiritual attributes, together with their talents, skills, creativity, and intellectual power, will not be at the disposal of the organization.
- Do not expect the impossible from workers. They are only human beings with many imperfections. They cannot perform like machines and it is unreasonable to demand of them to be perfect. After all, which manager is perfect in every aspect? This doesn't mean that sloppy work, laziness, or dishonesty should be condoned. Every organization must have certain performance standards and deviations from them cannot be tolerated. Certain tasks, of course, must be performed perfectly to be acceptable. A computer program, for instance, won't work if it contains bugs and other imperfections. But a little more compassion, understanding, leniency and tolerance in less important matters will give your concern a human face and make it people friendly.
- Do not expect too much from employees. Every person has a finite amount of time and energy available. When an emergency or a catastrophe occurs then it is, of course, acceptable to expect of people to do more than usual. But in ordinary times, employers and employees are bound by their contract of service and employers are precluded from expecting more that which has been agreed upon.

The Motivation of Workers

- Do not apply double standards. Workers can very easily see when management discriminates between employees or treats certain employees more favorably than others – for whatever reason. It is totally necessary to stay impartial and fair when dealing with discipline, punishment, promotion, and rewards. In other words: favoritism and discrimination of any sort is bad for any concern.
- Do not give contradictory or ambiguous orders. Such orders just cannot be executed and it is unfair and unreasonable to expect of workers to obey impossible demands. When somebody must perform an ambiguous role or two conflicting roles it creates unnecessary tension and stress. Therefore, be consistent and clear in all directives and orders and make sure that you are understood.
- Do not make promises you cannot keep. People expect those promises to be honored and when they are not kept disappointment and disillusionment will result. That is not good for productivity.

> *A group of five bus drivers consulted me. The company they had worked for employed them on a temporary basis. They were promised permanent positions after expiry of a probationary period. These permanent positions never materialized and they referred a case of unfair labor practices for arbitration. In the meantime, they got other employment, but they were also locked in costly legal battles with their former employer. They just cannot forget the fact that certain promises were not honored.*

- Do not be insensitive to personal problems that employees may have. When somebody has a sick child, marital problems, or an addiction, that will inevitably influence his or her work performance. It is counterproductive to put pressure on a worker who cannot perform adequately because of personal problems. It is much better to help such a person to visit a psychologist or social worker with whom these problems can be sorted out. Money invested in the counselling or psychotherapy of troubled employees will pay rich dividends in improved productivity.

WILL POWER

Since human beings have free will they can make choices and decisions. They have the ability to evaluate some possible courses of action and to prefer a certain option.

It is possible to analyze the factors that contribute to a person's motivation. The relative strengths of all his or her needs may be estimated or calculated, his or her personality and character make-up may be scrutinized and his or her beliefs and value systems may be investigated. But all this will never give a totally reliable and comprehensive explanation for that person's motives. There is always some or other hidden recess in that person's mind that defies investigation and explanation.

Some people are more able than others to stay with their original decisions. They are not so easily swayed by the opinions of others, group pressure, doubts, or new information and they carry on with whatever they had decided. In some cases, this may be seen as a manifestation of strong will power, although it might sometimes also be regarded as pig-headedness or plain stupidity. The best efforts to motivate people to become more productive may flounder on this phenomenon.

People are free agents and we can never pinpoint all the factors that influence their decisions and actions. Any manager should keep this in mind when the motivation of workers is an issue. It must be kept in mind that many workers are unproductive simply because they do not wish to be productive.

Will power
Watch! Stand firm in the faith! Be men! Be strong! (1 Cor 16: 13).

Strong-willed people usually make good leaders and good workers. They know what they want and how to get it. Obstacles and problems are seen as challenges or opportunities and they won't allow anybody or anything to deter them from reaching their chosen goals. They have the ability to get other people to follow their examples.

It is in an organization's interest to gain members' loyalty and willing co-operation. When all your best efforts to motivate or coerce them fail your last resort is to get them on your side and let them decide for themselves that what they really want is to work for you and do their best for you.

You will only be able to earn their loyalty and co-operation when you are scrupulously honest with them, when they know that they can rely on you, when it is evident that you are strong willed yourself and that your intentions with them are honest and honorable. So – harness the will power of people and help them to decide that what they want and desire is to be productive workers.

Chapter 5
Improving the Working Environment

Chapter Outline:
- *Working Conditions*
- *Human Relationships in the Organization*
- *The Culture of the Organization*
- *Pathological Cultures*
- *Policies and Practices of the Organization*
- *Leadership*
- *The Shape of the Organization*
- *Social Conditions of Employees*

The third group of factors which determines a worker's productivity is all the environmental factors which influence the work situation – the first and the second being the worker's abilities and his or her motivation. There are always environmental circumstances over which a worker has little or no control and which have an impact on his or her performance.

An extreme example of a situation where workers have no control over their work circumstances is where they are part of an assembly line. The speed of the assembly line determines the pace of work of all workers involved. Nobody can work faster or do more than usual since the assembly line moves at a predetermined speed. In this case, environmental factors place a ceiling on any worker's productivity.

One could divide environmental factors into internal and external factors. Internal factors are those that characterize the workplace or the enterprise, while external factors are those that come from without the organization. It is not possible to maintain a

The object of this chapter is, therefore, to give an overview of environmental factors, which may exert an influence on productivity, and to suggest ways and means to lessen the impact of unfavorable environmental conditions.

WORKING CONDITIONS

Although all the internal environmental factors to which workers are exposed may be classified as *working conditions*, in this chapter the term *working conditions* will be restricted to the following:

- Physical conditions;
- Remuneration;
- Working hours; and
- Ongoing training and the possibility of promotion.

- *Physical conditions*

Every worker is exposed to certain physical conditions. In certain cases, these conditions are necessarily unpleasant or dangerous and little can be done to improve these conditions:

o Seamen on a fishing trawler work in harsh conditions. They live in cramped quarters and they experience all sorts of adverse meteorological conditions – cold, heat, storms, and rough seas.
o Miners work in enclosed spaces and they must contend with heat, the danger of rockfalls and other hazards.
o Agricultural workers are exposed to the elements and they usually live far from towns and villages.
o Construction workers sometimes must work on high

Improving the Working Environment

and dangerous places such as bridges, towers, and high-rise buildings.

There is nothing that employers can do to ameliorate of soften these conditions. They are beyond the control of man. All that can be done is to provide workers with protective clothing and equipment and to assist them in other ways to cope as best as possible with these adverse conditions and dangers.

In most other cases it is, however, possible to do something to improve the physical conditions in which workers have to operate. There are legal requirements in most countries for creating safe working environments and employers can be forced to improve dangerous conditions.

A courier company whose drivers and crew members have experienced a hijacking and who are often traumatized by this experience, regularly send these workers to me for counselling. The trouble with this company is that its vehicles are clearly marked to advertise their services. However, this also causes these vehicles to be seen as targets by prospective hijackers and robbers who follow these vehicles and strike whenever they stop somewhere to deliver parcels. All these employees complain to me that they face unsafe working conditions.

In general, physical conditions, which are conducive to higher productivity, entail the following:

- There should be no exposure to hazards such as noxious gasses, corrosive fluids, deafening noises, falling objects, electrical shocks, radiation, radioactivity, or dangerous and faulty equipment;
- Equipment and furniture have to be comfortable and people-friendly;
- Working spaces should not be too cramped and should where feasible – afford a measure of privacy;
- Extreme temperatures should be avoided since that may affect a worker's attention and concentration;
- Buildings should be well maintained since untidy and badly painted offices and spaces tend to lower the morale of the workers;
- Loud or intermittent noises could detract a worker's attention or interfere with verbal communication;
- Distractions such as bad smells and flashing lights ought to be eliminated;
- Lighting and ventilation should be optimal; and
- The working environment may be improved by providing plants, works of art, and water features.

Special care should be taken of pregnant women and mothers with young children since they are more vulnerable than other people.

Certain concerns have found that the playing of soft and soothing music over the public address system, especially slow baroque music, affects the frame of mind of workers positively and helps them to concentrate better.

The science that deals with these aspects of work is called ergonomics. The aim of ergonomics is to create physical working conditions that are safe and comfortable. It stands to reason that employees cannot perform as expected when they are hampered by negative and uncomfortable conditions. Such conditions could lead to undue fatigue, loss of concentration, unnecessary mistakes, and accidents.

> *As a recruit, undergoing training in the Army, I had to stand guard on very cold winter nights at a fuel dump. The cold diminished my vigilance largely because the only thing I could think of was keeping warm. Fortunately, no saboteurs turned up, but if any intruders were to try anything, I surely would not have spotted them.*

Dangerous conditions can also have a detrimental effect on productivity in other ways. Miners who have experienced a life-threatening episode, such as a rock fall or a cave-in of a tunnel, may develop post-traumatic stress disorder, a psychological condition that is characterized by excessive anxiety, recurring nightmares, or flashbacks and an inability to concentrate. It becomes impossible for a worker who suffers from this condition to continue with his work and he has to be laid off due to medical reasons. The money invested in his training is thereby lost.

Many concerns have found that so-called telecommuting helps to improve productivity. Many workers live far from their workplaces and much time and energy are expended to commute daily to and from work. The Internet and fax machines have made it possible for certain categories of workers to do some or all their work at home and still stay in touch with headquarters. It is even possible for people to work for a firm in Stuttgart, Germany, while living in Gordon's Bay, South Africa. This practice became common during the Covid-19 pandemic in 2020 when people in many countries were forced to stay at home to prevent the spread of the virus. This habit has endured and many employees work mostly from home, visiting their offices infrequently.

- ***Remuneration***

When working conditions are mentioned people immediately tend to think of pay and other benefits. In the chapter dealing with motivation, much has already been said about monetary rewards for work.

A contract of service usually amounts to the following: An employee agrees to perform certain tasks and an employer agrees to pay him or her a certain amount of money in return. It is hard to conceptualize work without remuneration. Employers perform job evaluations to try and attach a certain monetary value on certain jobs. When a job is advertised the first thing a prospective candidate for that position wants to know is how much the salary is.

It is clear: if an employer is not prepared to pay his or her workers what they perceive what they are worth there will be trouble.

- ***Working Hours***

Working conditions include working hours. There are legal prescriptions in many countries on the amount of work an employer may expect from an employee, including over-time.

For instance: Section 7 of the Basic Conditions of Employment Act of 1997 of South Africa stipulates that employees are normally not allowed to work more than 45 hours per week.

That usually means a maximum of 8½ hours per day for a five-day week or 8 hours from Monday to Friday and 5 hours on Saturday.

The Act is, however, silent on starting times and flexible working times. Starting times for certain jobs may be uncomfortably early. More and more employers introduce flexible working hours, where it is feasible, to help employees manage their time more effectively.

Incumbents of certain other jobs often have to contend with changing shifts, which interrupt their sleeping patterns.

It is not possible to give a general rule on working hours to maximize productivity since the requirements and needs of firms and organizations differ so widely. Managers who are sensitive to productivity issues will undoubtedly investigate all possibilities and choose the option(s), which will have the best possible impact on productivity.

- *Ongoing training and the possibility of promotion*

When working conditions are mentioned, the possibility of further training and education and the possibility of being promoted are usually taken into account.

There are often legal prescriptions to entice employers to participate in the ongoing training of their workforce. The reason for this is the fact that a large percentage of the workforce in certain countries consists of unskilled and illiterate workers whose productivity is very low.

The attractiveness of a certain job is partly dependent upon the prospects of advancement. If people know that their hard work and dedication in an organization is to be rewarded by them being sent on courses to improve their skills and knowledge or by them being
given more senior positions, they will certainly be more willing to render better quality service.

The trend nowadays is to equip workers with a multitude of skills to be able to employ them in a variety of roles, instead of utilizing them only in a single function.

It sometimes happens that employees attend courses in various subjects at their own expense and in their own time. Examples are courses in financial management, human resources management, counselling, and book-keeping. Recognition for these accomplishments ought to be given by employers.

HUMAN RELATIONSHIPS IN THE ORGANIZATION

Adverse conditions in the workplace are usually the greatest source of stress which working people experience. Domestic problems are the second biggest source of stress for a working person.

Work-related stress stems in most cases from bad interpersonal relationships. These include clashes with co-workers, supervisors or management and conflict resulting from role uncertainty, role overload, role overlap and gaps in role assignment – together with a lack of social skills. The sexual harassment of female workers – where tolerated – is another serious source of stress and unhappiness.

- *Social skills*

Sound human relationships rest on good social or **interpersonal skills**. These skills can be described as –

> *the ability to produce the desired effect on others in a social situation.*

Social skills consist mainly of the following:

- Verbal skills (verbal fluency and listening skills); and
- Non-verbal skills (non-verbal communication, interpersonal attitudes, empathy, self-presentation, and assertiveness).

These skills can be taught. Training programs to improve the social skills of employees are always worthwhile – especially where employees must work together in teams or where they must deal with members of the public.

- *Conflict in the Work Situation*

Conflict can be described as –

> *the simultaneous occurrence of two or more incompatible motives or demands.*

That can lead to –

- frustration because goals cannot be reached or needs cannot be satisfied; and
- anger because people feel that they have been treated unjustly and unfairly – that is, their rights and interests were trampled upon.

Conflict in the workplace can either be constructive or destructive.

Constructive conflict, on the one hand, occurs in a controlled situation where people have different goals, plans, or expectations and where they can talk and argue in a civilized manner. This type of conflict can lead to innovative solutions of problems, challenges to workers to perform better and, indirectly, to improved productivity. This may happen during workshops, planning sessions, and team building exercises.

Destructive conflict, on the other hand, is bad for productivity. Destructive conflict may –

- lead to a waste of time and resources;
- be very costly in terms of unproductive energy expended;
- undermine peoples' psychological well-being; and
- result in sabotage of equipment or products by angry and frustrated workers.

When people have to work together while performing complex tasks it is inevitable that misunderstandings, hurt feelings, breakdowns in communication and destructive conflicts arise. These can have a detrimental effect on productivity and they ought to be managed properly. Conflict between individuals or groups within an organization may result from the following factors:

o Competition for scarce resources such as money, time, tools, materials, working space or transport;
o A clash of interests and the resulting bad feelings and distrust between individuals or groups;
o The abuse of workers by supervisors who are guilty of humiliating behavior or unreasonable punishment;
o Excessive control of workers by supervisors;

- Personality clashes resulting from differences regarding age, gender, work ethics, interests, etcetera;

  - The sexual harassment of female workers by their male colleagues; and
  - Competing demands from work, society, and home – many workers do not have enough time and energy to satisfy occupational as well as social and domestic demands and that causes friction at work and in the home.

The best policy is to prevent destructive conflict as much as possible. That can be achieved where sound and trusting relationships between all concerned parties are established. This happens where people are being recognized and respected as individuals – each with his or her own personality, needs, and rights. An enduring relationship is a relationship that is rewarding for all; all parties' social needs must be fulfilled and they must receive rewards such as recognition, security, and excitement.

Conflict is further avoided by sticking to the rules (formal and informal) regarding the relationships between supervisors and subordinates or between workers. A good example is the set of rules on sexual harassment that every employer is supposed to adopt. When these rules are transgressed, it should lead to disciplinary action to avoid a reoccurrence and to promote good relationships in the workplace.

Sometimes healthy competition between groups and teams within an organization deteriorates into rivalry and even hostility.

The only effective style for dealing with conflicts within an organization is the co-operative style. The maximum effort must be made to satisfy the needs of everybody and to get all the parties satisfied. This calls for an in-depth investigation into the real needs, rights and interests of the parties and creative solutions to satisfy those needs, rights, and interests. These solutions may result in some adaptations by certain parties but everybody will gain by having improved relationships between the competing factions.

The co-operative style of dealing with conflict utilizes one or more of the following techniques:

- o Letting off steam – the affected parties get the opportunity to state their case and to voice their frustrations and anger; when they perceive that their concerns are being heard it may lead to greater calm and rationality;
- o Negotiation – the warring factions are encouraged to listen to each other and to try to understand the views of the other side to weed out spurious and unrealistic demands;
- o Confrontation – the competing parties undertake an honest investigation into the reasons for the conflict and to find common ground; this must lead –
    - to plans to overcome the clash of interests;
    - to a solution acceptable to all parties; and
    - to a clear undertaking by the parties to co-operate in future; and
    - Appeal to a higher authority and arbitration – an impartial person or group of persons in a position of authority are to investigate the causes for the conflict and make a ruling, which is binding on all those affected.

Improving the Working Environment

> *Peacemakers*
> Blessed are the peacemakers, for they shall be called sons of God (Matt 5: 9).

- **Role-Related Stress**

Every job and every position imply that the incumbent assume certain roles. A manager has, for instance, to be a good leader, innovator, administrator, counsellor, mentor, and communicator.

It is not always clear which roles a certain person must play and role ambiguity may occur, which causes stress. The person may have to improvise – especially in a new job. This may not always meet with the approval of others and conflict may result.

Friction can also arise from role conflict. That happens where tasks and relationships are not articulated (and this is not always possible) and where the job incumbent and others in the environment (supervisors, colleagues *etcetera*) have differring perceptions of the roles connected with the job. These conflicting perceptions and expectations may lead to stress and conflict.

The management of this type of conflict calls for great wisdom. A round table conference under the chairmanship of a senior manager or personnel officer where all concerned parties can voice their concerns, frustrations, problems, needs, and expectations can do a lot to diffuse a difficult situation.

Another source of conflict is role overlap. This happens where the same role or task is assigned to two different employees or teams. Each will see the other's actions as an invasion into personal territory or sphere of influence and that will cause resentment.

The opposite situation, that of gaps in role assignment, is also a cause of friction. Where workers are dependent on each other for the completion of their tasks, but certain necessary steps in the process are not assigned to anybody, then these workers will certainly blame each other for letting the other down.

The remedy for conflict resulting from role overlap and gaps in role assignment is, of course, a thorough job analysis of all jobs concerned, a better definition of roles, and a clear and definitive demarcation of boundaries.

- *Social Skills Training*

Conflict in the work place can be largely avoided where the social skills of managers, supervisors, and employees are improved by training. The best method has proved to be a combination of role-play and lectures, video or film presentations and discussions.

During role-play real life situations are mimicked and afterwards analyzed and criticized by the audience. The course leader, usually a social scientist, uses this role-play to give coaching in various subjects. Many studies have confirmed the success of this type of training: managers learn to manage better, supervisors learn to supervise better, and workers learn to work more effectively and efficiently.

The following subjects are usually covered:

- human relations (the giving of recognition, dealing with emotional and aggressive people *etcetera*);
- general management;
- self-awareness and self-presentation;

- knowledge of the cultural diversity of South Africa;
- communication skills;
- problem solving;
- motivation;
- negotiation, facilitating conflict and group dynamics; and
- disciplinary action and the handling of complaints.

THE CULTURE OF THE ORGANIZATION

When the word *culture* is mentioned most people tend to think of art such as music, architecture, sculpture, poetry etc. These forms of art certainly are aspects of the culture of a society, but culture is a much wider and broader concept. It has to do with the values, traditions, beliefs, and relationships prevalent in that society. These can be expressed by means of art, but they are more usually manifest in the life style and behavioral patterns of the people.

o *Corporate culture*

Organizations are also characterized by their own cultures. An **organization's culture** – also called corporate culture – can be described as:

> *the way things are being done by the members of that organization,*
> or
> *the values, goals, traditions, assumptions, beliefs, attitudes, rituals, and relationships, which characterize that organization and help to establish its identity.*

These values, goals, traditions, assumptions, beliefs, attitudes, rituals, and relationships are usually taken for granted and are not always well articulated. They, nevertheless, exert a powerful influence over the work behavior of the members of the organization.

The culture of an organization is transmitted and perpetuated by the example set by influential members of the organization. The way they usually do things and their comments on events set the trend and that is emulated by other members of the organization. Every organization has, furthermore, certain stories, myths, and legends about important events in the past. These stories explain the values of the organization and the way things are being done. The culture is usually initiated by the founders of the organization who deemed it necessary to do things in a certain manner and that sets the trend for the future.

In a large organization, subcultures are likely. Different departments or sections will have their own ways of doing things whereby their identity is emphasized.

Cultures may be strong or weak. In a small and young organization, it is to be expected that the members will not be as attached to the core values and traditions of the organization as in a large and older organization. The stronger and more entrenched a given culture is, the more stable it will be; and efforts to change it will meet with resistance.

It is extremely difficult to merge two cultures. When one firm is taken over by another and their cultures are widely divergent then the merger will certainly cause much resentment and friction since people will not be very willing to adopt new values, strategies, and relationships.

> *The elections for local authorities in South Africa at the end of 2000 resulted in the merger of many local authorities into greater units. The area of authority of the new Municipality of the Unicity of Cape Town, for instance, incorporated several previously independent municipalities from Gordon's Bay in the south to Atlantis in the north. The new city council decided with great wisdom not to merge these units in one go but to spread the process out over a number of years. The city council faced a tremendous challenge, namely to create a new culture for the new Unicity.*
>
> *The present South African National Defense Force is the result of a merger of the previous South African Defense Force, the forces of the previous so-called homelands and the military wings of former liberation movements. At the time of writing, more than thirty years after the merger, it seems as if the clash of cultures within the SANDF may be something of the past. Many competent officers of the old SADF left the service because they could not handle this clash of cultures. A few tragic incidents, such as soldiers who went on shooting sprees that hit the headlines demonstrate the fact that this merger of cultures was not always proceeding smoothly.*

- **Cultural Dimensions**

The culture of any enterprise or organization usually deals with the following issues:

- o The identity of the organization;
- o The organization's place in the world and its relationship with the environment;
- o A frame of reference for interpreting events within and without the organization;

Improving the Working Environment

- The extent to which members of the organization identify with the organization as a whole;
- The way employees are treated, penalized, and rewarded;
- The way clients and customers are treated;
- The importance given to the evaluation and assessment of employees;
- The importance given to the development and the careers of employees;
- The way in which members who retire or quit are treated;
- The way decisions are made and how much decision-making authority and autonomy are given to juniors;
- The extent to which supervisors and managers interfere with the work of their subordinates or give them support;
- How rigid or how flexible the organizational structure is;
- The way in which risks and challenges are assessed and approached;
- The way in which the administration of the concern is handled; and
- Whether the concern sticks to its main business or ventures out into new fields.

The culture of any organization plays an important role in the day-to-day running of that organization. If managers, supervisors, and other employees have internalized the values and beliefs of the concern, they need less control since they can be counted upon to act and behave in a certain manner.

There is no question that the culture of some organizations can be bad for productivity. If it is, for instance, acceptable that customers are to be treated with disrespect, that the opinions of junior employees count for nothing, and that absolutely no risks are to be taken, then it may be expected that productivity will be low.

A culture that is conducive to high productivity is a culture that meets the challenges of the external environment, that fits the organization's goals with the strategy of the organization, and that is aligned with the available technology. It is necessary that management regularly conduct a cultural diagnosis to determine whether the current culture is appropriate.

PATHOLOGICAL CULTURES

An organization's culture may be seen as that organization's personality, just as every individual person also has his or her own personality.

A person is more than a conglomerate of body parts and organs. He or she is a unique entity and that unity and uniqueness is brought about by having a definite personality. Likewise, an organization as an entity is also something that is more or bigger than the sum total of its constituent parts. This "more" comprises *inter alia* its culture – together with its structure, shape, and internal relationships.

Every person has some personality flaws. We regard that as normal since no person is perfect. These flaws may, however, become pathological and that person may suffer from a personality disorder, a mood disorder, or a psychosis. Organizations may also develop pathological personalities or cultures.

Researchers have identified the following types of pathological corporate cultures:

- ***The Anti-Social Organization:***

This organization has no respect for the rule of law and disregards the human rights of clients and employees, including the right not to be discriminated against or the right not to be subjected to sexual harassment.

- ***The Narcissistic Organization:***

This organization has an over-inflated view of its own importance and thinks that the rest of the world exists to serve its interests. It regards clients as an unavoidable evil who disturb the organization's peace.

- ***The Depressed Organization:***

This type of organization interprets events in the darkest colors possible. Everything is seen as a potential danger or calamity and absolutely no risks are taken.

- ***The Hyperactive Organization:***

The members of this type of organization are extremely busy. They have only one motivation for all their activities, and that is to impress the boss – not to satisfy the client.

- ***The Compulsive Organization:***

This type of organization is unwilling to learn from its mistakes and keeps on repeating the same mistakes in a compulsive manner.

- ***The Schizophrenic Organization:***

This organization has lost touch with reality and creates its own reality. It doesn't try to ascertain what the customers want or need and how technology has changed, but lives in its own world and stays busy with its own inner workings.

- **The Paranoid Organization:**

The prevalent culture in this type of organization is that of distrust and suspicion. Everybody, including the organization's own members, is suspected of plotting to harm the organization.

It is almost unnecessary to say that organizations with any of these cultures are doomed. These pathological cultures make their survival extremely unlikely – unless these cultures are changed.

A Sick Culture

To the angel of the assembly in Laodicea write: "The Amen, the Faithful and True Witness, the Head of God's creation, says these things: "I know your works, that you are neither cold nor hot. I wish you were cold or hot. So, because you are lukewarm, and neither hot nor cold, I will vomit you out of my mouth. Because you say, `I am rich, and have gotten riches, and have need of nothing;` and don't know that you are the wretched one, miserable, poor, blind, and naked; I counsel you to buy from me gold refined by fire, that you may become rich; and white garments, that you may clothe yourself, and that the shame of your nakedness may not be revealed; and eye salve to anoint your eyes, that you may see. As many as I love, I reprove and chasten. Be zealous therefore, and repent (Rev 3: 14–19).

- **Changing A Culture**

If management is concerned about substandard productivity and the negative influence of certain aspects of the firm's culture on productivity then there are basically three strategies to follow.

- ***The first option is to manage the existing culture and take advantage of the existing values and traditions.***

That means that management should know exactly which values and traditions are prevalent and which behavior rests upon these values. This knowledge can only be acquired by being part of the organization for a certain length of time and having one's ear to the ground. The positive aspects of the culture must then be emphasized, encouraged, and rewarded to such an extent that the less positive aspects become unimportant and eventually vanish.

The reverse can also be tried. Management could make it clear that certain attitudes and behaviors will in future be unacceptable. This has to be made part of the organization's ethical code and disciplinary policy. When people are caught in the act and found guilty in a fair hearing of transgressing the new values and norms, certain sanctions may be imposed upon them, beginning with verbal and written warnings. It is important that these measures be applied consistently and fairly. It will certainly be counterproductive if managers and supervisors continue to set bad examples while other employees are being punished for the same behavior.

This strategy must be applied with great circumspection because it certainly will cause resentment and resistance. Punishing bad behavior must always be accompanied by rewarding good behavior.

- ***The second strategy is to actively assist the socialization process of new members of the organization.***

New members must be taught the ropes before they can start to operate independently and productively. It is easy for them to pick up bad habits when they observe bad examples most of the time. Often a mentor is assigned to a new member to help him or her to adjust to the new environment and to show him or her around. If this mentor can teach the new member the good values and beliefs of the organization's culture then the chances are that that person will be less likely to pick up bad habits.

- ***The third option is to try and change the organization's culture and eliminate the less desirable elements thereof.***

This is easier said than done since cultures become deeply entrenched over time and resist change. It is always easier to revert to certain habits in certain situations than to think rationally about what the outcome of a certain course of action would be.

The best way is to stage some sort of crisis. When an organization faces a crisis then change and adaptation is more likely. The crisis that is to be staged must be visible to all members. Such crises can be created by replacing the top echelon of the management team, by reorganizing and scrambling the structure of the organization and by widespread retrenchments. These crises will send out the message that things cannot continue along old paths and that a reappraisal of goals, strategies, habits, and methods is necessary. This must be accompanied by a well-publicized reformulation of the concern's vision and mission.

Together with this, management ought to create new stories and myths by staging or organizing certain events, situations, rituals, and incidents to illustrate the new values and beliefs. When an influential member of the organization, preferably the chief executive, deliberately behaves counter to the existing culture it certainly will cause a stir. The story of the incident will be told and retold and when that member persists in behaving in that way a new tradition can be established. It is important not to inadvertently revert to the old ways because that will re-establish and strengthen the old culture.

Improving the Working Environment

Since cultures are resistant to change, it will not be an easy task to carry through. Organizations who change their culture usually need a minimum of two years to accomplish this. All the strategies mentioned above need to be implemented simultaneously and consistently to achieve results.

A firm that succeeds in weeding out negative aspects of its culture and cultivating the more positive aspects will certainly succeed in improving productivity. These new positive aspects of the culture will prove to be just as resilient and enduring as the old negative aspects, which had to be changed with great difficulty.

It is desirable that firms develop a culture –

- in which previously powerless workers are empowered;
- where the human rights of all members of the organization are respected;
- of tolerance and mutual respect between the sexes and between members of different racial, cultural, and religious groups;
- where good manners and civility are encouraged;
- where there is a sensitivity for the needs of the external environment;
- in which the satisfaction of the customer is of prime importance; and

- where superior performance and high productivity are held in high regard.

Perhaps the easiest and most effective way of establishing a culture of excellent performance in an organization is to design an effective appraisal system. When employees know that their performance and outputs are to be monitored, they are more likely to do their best and work efficiently and effectively. If management isn't interested in the performance of its employees, then these employees will also show little interest in delivering good work.

POLICIES AND PRACTICES OF THE ORGANIZATION

Something that is related to the culture of an organization is the policies and practices of an organization. No organization can function without definite and well-articulated policies, rules, plans, and procedures. In addition, every organization must have its own vision (its ultimate goal), its own mission (the reason for its existence), its own slogan (a short statement of policy), its own values and its own code of conduct.

---

*The **slogan** of the **University of Stellenbosch** is: "Your knowledge partner".*

*The **vision statement** of the University states:*

"Stellenbosch University –
- *Is an academic institution of excellence and a respected knowledge partner;*
- *Contributes towards building the scientific, technological, and intellectual capacity of Africa*

> - *Is an active role-player in the development of the South African society;*
> - *Has a campus culture that welcomes a diversity of people and ideas;*
> - *Promotes Afrikaans as a language of teaching and science in a multilingual context."*
>
> The **mission statement** of the University is as follows:
>
> *"The raison d'être of the University of Stellenbosch is to create and sustain, in commitment to the academic ideal of excellent scholarly and scientific practice, an environment within which knowledge can be discovered, can be shared, and can be applied to the benefit of the community."*
>
> The University subscribes to the following **values**:
>
> - *Equity;*
> - *Participation;*
> - *Transparency;*
> - *Readiness to serve;*
> - *Tolerance and mutual respect;*
> - *Dedication;*
> - *Scholarship;*
> - *Responsibility; and*
> - *Academic Freedom.*

Some aspects of the policies of organizations are regulated by legislation. No company may adopt financial policies that clash with the laws of the country. Personnel policy is regulated by existing labor legislation.

The policy that has the most direct bearing on the day-to-day running of an organization and the work performance of employees is arguably the disciplinary policy and code of that organization. It is therefore necessary that any employer formulate this policy and code as extensively and clearly as possible. This policy and code should describe which actions and behaviors are unacceptable or dangerous and what the penalties for transgressions are. The procedures to be followed in cases of disciplinary action are to be articulated fully.

It is necessary that disciplinary procedures are applied fairly and consistently, otherwise morale in the organization will inevitably suffer. When workers have the perception that management acts inconsistently and unfairly then confidence in the management will decline and productivity will suffer. Any form of favoritism or discrimination on any ground is, therefore, bad for discipline and productivity.

Management must, in addition, be seen to uphold the adopted code of ethics and set a correct example for the rest of the organization. If management does not take the code of ethics seriously then it cannot be expected of the work force to take it seriously, either.

Disciplinary hearings should be conducted along the following lines:

- The supervisor or manager finds out as much as possible about the purported misconduct or unsatisfactory performance of an accused employee and decides on a strategy to be followed. It must be decided whether the purported transgression merits an informal hearing, a formal hearing, or may be ignored.
- If the alleged offence is of a less serious nature an interview is scheduled and the supervisor/manager gives the employee time to prepare for the interview. When the interview starts the

supervisor or manager talks to the employee and tries to get the atmosphere as relaxed as possible to enable the employee to talk freely and with confidence.
- The problem should then be explained and facts such as statistics, reports etcetera should be presented. The employee must be invited to respond and explain his or her actions.
- Thereafter, possible solutions are explored jointly to ensure the employee's co-operation.
- At the end, the supervisor/manager gives a summary of findings and promises made and these are confirmed in writing.
- After the interview, the supervisor/manager must monitor the employee's progress and conduct. If there is no improvement further interviews must be scheduled with the possible imposition of sanctions, which may eventually result in dismissal.
- If the allegations made against an employee are of a serious nature, such as theft, dishonesty, assault on a fellow worker or intoxication during working hours, then a full investigation in the accused's presence is called for. The accused must be informed of the charges against him or her and he or she ought to be afforded ample time to prepare a defense. The accused may be assisted by a fellow employee or a trade union representative. In serious cases the accused may even be represented by a legal representative. During the hearing the parties may call witnesses and cross-examine the witnesses of the other party. Documentary evidence may also be presented. The accused must be afforded ample opportunity to state his or her case.
- The hearing ought to be chaired by an independent or impartial person – in some cases somebody from outside the organization. The organization may be represented by a senior

employee or a manager. Written reasons for the ultimate finding should be given. If the employee is found guilty of a serious breach of discipline, a summary dismissal is warranted.

Another aspect of company policy that has a bearing on productivity is the policy on the advancement and promotion of employees. It is the ideal that everybody should know that a worker's chances of promotion rest solely on merit and the availability of positions and not on favoritism or company politics.

It is necessary to stress that all members of an organization should be well informed about the vision, mission, slogan, and value statement of the organization and that they support it. When that is the case, the organization's policies will find acceptance and they will become part of the corporate culture.

ETHICAL LEADERSHIP

In two previous chapters, the impact of good and inspiring leadership on motivation and performance was discussed. There are, though, more to leadership than that and, therefore, the theme of leadership has to be examined further.

- *Managers And Leaders*

The trend nowadays is to move away from management and replace it with leadership. Workers are more sophisticated than in the past and they are more aware of their human rights. The authoritarian culture of the past is not acceptable anymore and therefore traditional management has to be replaced by a more democratic set-up in the workplace. Ordinary workers demand to know more about the way organizations are being run and they expect more transparency.

That does not mean that the workers should be running factories, mines, and other enterprises. What it does mean is that employers must learn to accept employees as responsible partners whose inputs and comments are to be valued and welcomed. Of course, functions such as supervision, planning, co-ordination, financial control, decision-making, delegation, and organizing are still necessary. What has to change, though, is the style in which these functions are to be performed.

The days of rigid organizational structures are over. It should be the organization's stated policy to be as flexible and adaptable as possible. One way of achieving this is by instituting near-autonomous teams which are united by a shared vision, goals, and culture (more of this later).

Organizations of the 21st century function much better where responsibilities and decision-making power is shared by as many people as possible, even down to the lowest grades. It should be policy to invite every member to present comments, criticism, and suggestions regarding the running of the concern. It should be policy to encourage all members to experiment, innovate and create new systems and procedures.

It is not enough to inform the workforce of decisions taken by management; they must be drawn into the decision-making process. Workers should have the autonomy to make their own decisions within the parameters of company policy and to inform their superiors accordingly. This will make a complex system of supervision and management redundant since workers will become their own supervisors and managers where they are treated as mature and responsible people.

It is a truism that the productivity of a company and its workers depends on the way management goes about its business. An element of any working environment is the type of leadership workers receive and it is necessary to investigate how leadership in the workplace influences productivity.

- **_The Quality Of Supervision_**

In any sizeable enterprise, there are several levels of supervision. Supervisors or team leaders usually perform the first line of supervision. Junior managers, middle managers, and senior managers take care of the other levels. All of them are supervisors, though their supervisory functions differ, depending on the level they occupy.

The task of supervising comprises the following two functions:

- o The supervisor must see that the work is being done properly and that productivity is being kept up; and
- o The supervisor must look after the welfare of his or her subordinates and help to improve their work satisfaction.

This task of supervision is usually one of the items on a supervisor's or manager's job description. Apart from supervision, supervisors and managers usually have other managerial, administrative, or technical functions to fulfil. Supervisors are usually appointed as such since they are good at the jobs of the persons over whom they were appointed.

A supervisor must be a good communicator. Any good leader keeps his or her followers informed of plans and decisions and communicates their problems and concerns to the appropriate authorities and powers in the organization. It has been found that when there is good communication from supervisors and management to the workers it has a positive influence on job satisfaction and work performance and keeps labor turnover low.

It is also very desirable that supervisors and managers keep workers informed about the goals and objectives of the organization, of their department, and of their team, about the successes, acquisitions, losses and failures of the organization and its constituent parts and about all changes which are taking place. It is also important to communicate information about the contributions and successes of individual workers.

Supervision is an art that can be taught and learnt. Good supervisors and managers have, therefore, to be trained to perform their duties efficiently and humanely. They must be trained to handle conflict between workers, to conduct appraisals, and disciplinary hearings properly and fairly and to give counseling and guidance to workers who need it.

The quality of supervision has a direct bearing on productivity. If supervision is slack, workers will be tempted to under-perform, malinger, or be dishonest. If supervision is of a high quality, workers will be made proud of their achievements and their motivation will be higher.

It is popular to distinguish between task-oriented and people-oriented leaders. It is a useful distinction, if it is remembered that these descriptions do not denote opposites. A leader can be both task-oriented and people-oriented at the same time – as has been pointed out previously.

This state of affairs has to do with the dual task of any supervisor to see that the work is being done and that the welfare of his or her subordinates is served. It has been found that productivity is highest when supervisors score high on both tasks or on task-orientation. When the supervisor scores low on the dimension of looking after the interests of his or her subordinates, job satisfaction usually suffers.

Extremes are to be avoided, though. When a supervisor scores extremely high on task-orientation and very low on people-orientation productivity falls and complaints against that supervisor increase sharply because of his or her dictatorial style.

- **_Participatory Leadership_**

Supervisors can also be either authoritarian or less autocratic. The trend is towards participatory leadership, which is a more democratic style. This means that decisions are explained to the group or even taken by the group or team under the leadership of the supervisor. The leader considers the fact that group members are individuals who differ from each other and that everyone can play a constructive role in performing the tasks and projects assigned to the group. This strategy ensures greater acceptance of decisions by the group and a higher commitment to achieve the goals of the group.

Effective and democratic leaders have clear goals and they inspire their followers to share those goals. They are, furthermore, sensitive to the welfare of their followers, are experts in the field in which the organization operates, are quality-oriented and they can utilize rewards and punishment effectively. Good leaders understand the art of asking and requesting in such a manner that it does not sound like threatening, begging, or demanding.

There is a limit, though. Where a supervisor becomes too democratic and thereby relinquishes his or her role as leader, the result will be anarchy where everybody does what he or she likes.

There are several rules which democratic supervisors should apply to perform their task properly. These rules are, briefly, the following:

- Plan and assign tasks efficiently;
- Keep subordinates informed of all decisions;

- Explain the reason for orders or decisions;
- Consult subordinates in matters that affect them;
- Encourage the development and advancement of subordinates;
- Respect the right to privacy, dignity, and other human rights of subordinates;
- Help subordinates with their personal problems;
- Represent subordinates and their interests in the wider organization; and
- Do not supervise too closely – this interferes with work efficiency.

o *Leadership Skills*

People can be trained to be effective leaders. The notion that good leaders are born as leaders is not accepted anymore. There are several skills which can be taught and which good leaders need to do a god job of leading, supervising and managing:

o Leaders need verbal communication skills. They must be able to give clear and concise instructions, explanations, and requests, ask the right questions to obtain information and give on-the-job training. Good communication entails the following:

- Communicate on the level of the person who is spoken to;
- Make sure that the message is being received;
- Make sure that the other person knows how and when to respond or to report back;
- Communicate clearly what must be done, how it must be done, how well it must be done, where it must be done and when the task must be completed.

Improving the Working Environment

- o Leaders need non-verbal communication skills. They must have the right social attitudes, appropriate emotions, adequate self-presentation, and assertiveness.
- o Managers need to have the skills to conduct various types of interviews: selection interviews, appraisal interviews, grievance hearings and disciplinary hearings.

- o Participatory leadership requires, in addition, the following skills: the ability to lead a group to consensus, the ability to listen, the ability to handle conflict, the ability to delegate tasks, the ability to give feed-back, and the ability to evaluate others' performance.
- o Managers and supervisors need to know how to chair meetings. The following rules are useful:

    - Come prepared by studying the agenda thoroughly and doing some research beforehand;
    - Know the procedures to be followed;
    - Know the names of all the participants;
    - Know how to deal with difficult (talkative and aggressive) members of the meeting; the most effective is to let the other members of the meeting silence them;
    - Give everybody a chance to take part in deliberations but prevent a situation where two or more persons speak at the same time;

- Know how to save time;
- It is desirable to lead a meeting to consensus instead of taking a vote;
- Use visual aids to illustrate a point or explain a difficult concept; and
- Make a summary and draw conclusions at the end of a discussion to bring it to a close.

Good Leadership

When the righteous thrive, the people rejoice; But when the wicked rule, the people groan (Prov 29: 2).

You know that the rulers of the Gentiles lord it over them, and their great ones exercise authority over them. It shall not be so among you, but whoever would become great among you will be your servant. Whoever would be first among you will be your bondservant (Matt 20: 25–27).

THE SHAPE OF THE ORGANIZATION

One of the important constituents of any working environment is the shape and size of the organization.

- ***Organizational Structures***

Organizations come in all shapes and sizes, depending on –
- age – older organizations tend to be bigger than younger ones;
- the type of business pursued – a workshop for motor repairs will necessary be smaller than a steel factory or a chemical plant and will have a much simpler organizational structure;
- technology utilized – usually only bigger firms can afford state-of-the-art technology; this state-of-the-art technology mostly requires highly trained personnel and they will be organized differently from a gang of semi-skilled workers;

-
- location – a firm operating in the desert regions of Namaqualand or the Karoo will tend to be smaller than one operating in Johannesburg or the Cape Peninsula in South Africa;
- type of clientele catered for – big businesses tend to deal with other big organizations instead of with smaller firms or individuals; and
- turnover.

The shape of an organization is largely dependent on its size. Small organizations will of necessity have a simpler and more informal organizational structure and fewer levels of authority than larger organizations. Large concerns tend to have centralized authority, rigid chains of command and more rules regulating the relationships between individuals and between departments.

Repeated studies have found that job satisfaction and productivity is higher in smaller firms and organizations. Smaller firms also tend to have a lower accident rate, lower labor turnover and less labor unrest. Many big organizations have decentralized for this reason. Departments, sections, and teams were given greater autonomy and decision-making power, as well as a better-defined role within the larger whole.

It is necessary that a thorough organizational diagnosis be undertaken to ascertain where organizational structures hinder productivity, create conflict, and prevent cost-effective operations. The points mentioned above which determine the shape and size of an organization must be considered to determine whether the organization is structured optimally. This is a task for which an expert and a consultant who specializes in organizational theory will have to be called in.

Where it becomes apparent that changes in the organizational structure are necessary, these changes should be introduced with great circumspection. Just as changes in corporate culture meet with resistance, so management can expect resistance against organizational changes since these may threaten the influence, status, job level, or job security of certain people. An outside agent, such as a consultant, will also be necessary to facilitate this process.

Iscor's steel mill in Vanderbijlpark, South Africa, managed to lower production costs and to improve productivity by 28% between 1994 and 2001. This has been achieved by introducing new technology, but also by reorganizing the workforce. The structure of the organization was drastically overhauled by reducing the number of grades within the organization from 190 to 47 and by halving the number of employees. Severance packages were offered to all members older than 55.

Any organization should function as an integrated and unified system. Systems usually comprise several interdependent subsystems. It goes without saying that these subsystems should assist each other in a co-ordinated way instead of becoming embroiled in strife and conflict.

Industrial organizations are comprised of technical subsystems and social subsystems. The technical subsystem has as sub-subsystems technology (tools and plants), raw materials and production methods for transforming the raw materials into finished products by means of the technology. The social subsystem consists of the sub-subsystems of management and employees (organized into departments, sections, and teams), as well as the relationships between these parts and the roles all the groups and individuals have to fulfil.

Social systems are usually open to the environment and certain sections of the environment (the government with its laws, suppliers, competitors, clients, new technology etcetera) have a measure of influence over these systems. Any social system must be unified by a common vision and shared values, methods, and goals.

A system is doomed if its unity is broken. That may happen where members of certain groups within the organization (departments, teams, ethnic groups, or occupational groups) see other groups as competitors instead of allies. Groups may form coalitions with other groups against the rest of the organization in a quest for more resources or power and it is the task of management to prevent this from happening.

It will always be difficult to make all subsystems work efficiently together, especially in a growing and developing organization. No department or group changes at the same rate and in the same direction as the rest of the organization and a measure of divergence is usually to be expected.

- ***The Composition Of Teams***

Most workplaces are staffed by a number of employees and supervisors who have to work together. They are usually organized into teams, groups, divisions, departments, or sections – each with its own internal organization. Some teams are assembled only for a specific task or project while other groups are more or less permanent.

It is obvious that the selection of teams and the composition of groups cannot be left to chance. If people with the wrong skills or incompatible personalities are dumped together in proximity it may spell disaster. Numerous investigations have confirmed that work performance suffers when colleagues and team members cannot get along with each other. Therefore, the formation of the social working environment needs careful consideration and planning.

Teams are sometimes assembled for a certain project or task and they may be disbanded after completion of that project or task. The members of such a team are usually selected only on the grounds of the skills needed for the task on hand and their availability. Sometimes, a team leader is appointed and he is tasked with the selection of team members from a pool of available workers.

Since these team members must work in proximity, have to co-ordinate their efforts and are dependent on each other it is very necessary that the selection of the team members receive special consideration and that they be trained to work together. Their personalities, level of motivation, value systems and disciplinary records should receive consideration.

> *The Value of Teamwork*
> Two are better than one, because they have a good reward for their labor. For if they fall, the one will lift up his fellow; but woe to him who is alone when he falls, and doesn't have another to lift him up. Again, if two lie together, then they have warmth; but how can one keep warm alone? If a man prevails against one who is alone, two shall withstand him; and a threefold cord is not quickly broken (Eccl 4: 9 – 12).

High-performing teams usually exhibit an overall team purpose, mutual accountability, collective work products, shared leadership roles, high cohesiveness and group loyalty, collaboration in choosing procedures, collective task assignment, and collective assessment of their own successes and failures.

The cohesiveness of a team can be improved by team building exercises where the necessary skills are taught and where members learn to trust each other. During team building exercises teams ought to get greater clarity on the following questions:

- Who are we?
- What are our tasks?
- Which skills and aptitudes are available?
- How are we to perform our work?

- How do we know when we perform as expected?
- Are there better methods for performing our tasks?
- How can we improve?
- How can we enjoy our team more?

The success of a team is dependent on the following:

- A supportive environment;
- Clear objectives and goals;
- A clear division of tasks and roles; and
- Enough opportunity for communication and interaction.

A successful team has the following attributes:

- A clear vision of the future which inspires everybody;
- A clear goal which is pursued by all members of the team;
- Clarity on who are members of the team and who are not;
- Strong leadership by an inspired and competent leader;
- Enjoyment by members of their membership of the team and willing co-operation;
- Mutual trust;
- Collective ownership and responsibility for the outputs of the team;
- Consensus on values, roles, plans of action and working methods;

- Good communication within the team and with the environment;
- The necessary skills and knowledge to successfully perform the tasks assigned to the team;
- Flexibility and the willingness to learn new skills and adopt new procedures;
- A willingness to improve performance; and
- Internal management of all matters pertaining to the team.

It is necessary that teams operate on the basis of consensus. Consensus may be reached in one or more of the following ways:

- Everybody agrees;
- Everybody agrees to differ;
- Only those team members or subgroups who are influenced by the outcome of a decision participate in the decision-making process;
- When votes are taken the minority agrees to abide by the decision of the majority; or
- Everybody agrees that those with dissenting votes should come with practical alternative plans or courses of action.

- ***Levels of Authority***

It is possible that an organization may be over-managed by having too many levels of authority. Such a top-heavy conglomerate will be sluggish, unproductive, and unprofitable. As a simple rule of thumb, it may be stated that the span of command of any supervisor or manager should not be more than twelve individuals. This implies:

- For every 10 – 12 workers there should be a supervisor;
- For every 4 – 6 supervisors there should be a junior manager (who may have his or her own administrative staff to make up the number of ten to twelve individuals);
- For every 4 – 6 junior managers there should be a middle manager (who may have his or her own administrative and support staff);
- For every 4 – 6 middle managers there should be a senior manager (who may have his or her own administrative and support staff, including a second-in-command);
- For an organization with branches and departments in different parts of the country there should be one national manager. The number of levels beneath him or her depends on the sizes of the different branches and departments and the total size of the organization as a whole.

It seems that five levels of command are adequate for a nation-wide organization. Smaller concerns will do well with fewer levels.

The higher levels of command are more concerned with the strategy of the organization while the lower levels are more concerned with the operational aspects of the organization. That means that middle managers and senior managers make decisions concerning the future while the decisions of junior managers, supervisors, and workers impact mainly on immediate problems and challenges.

It is a sign of a healthy organization –

- when employees, supervisors, and managers are empowered to take decisions, which need not to be taken at higher levels; and o when the members of the organization are used to be held accountable for their decisions and actions and they accept the responsibilities bestowed upon them.

A distinction should be made between line managers and support staff. Line managers manage the operational department(s) of the organization and they have the authority to hold those under them accountable for their decisions and actions. These operational department(s) hold the bulk of the employees and carry on the main business or operations of the concern.

Support personnel man the staff departments. These are typically the personnel department, the marketing department, the procurement department, the financial department, the planning or development department, and the maintenance department. The functions performed by these departments may be outsourced to outside agencies and consultants. Administrative personnel are also found in the offices of line managers.

The level of the heads of the staff departments will always be on a lower level than that of the top manager. The level of the members of these departments will depend on their responsibilities, qualifications, professional status and expertise and they will, in most cases, be on a higher level than that of the bulk of ordinary workers in the operational departments.

The Army may be taken as an example of the principles mentioned above:
A division, consisting of infantry, armor, artillery, and other branches, is supposed to be organized along the following lines:
- *The smallest unit in the infantry is the squad consisting of about ten soldiers. In the artillery and the armor the basic units*

- *are gun crews and tank or armored car crews. Their supervisors are corporals and lance-corporals.*
- *Three infantry squads usually form a platoon and four tanks, four armored cars and four artillery crews form a troop. The junior managers at this level are the platoon/troop leaders (a lieutenant and a sergeant). They usually have control over six to eight supervisors.*
- *A company, battery or squadron is comprised of three or more platoons or troops and they are commanded by a major, a captain as second-in-command and a company/battery/squadron sergeant major. They are also to be regarded as junior managers. They manage six or more junior managers on a lower level.*
- *Four or more companies of infantry, squadrons of armor or batteries of artillery, together with a headquarters company with supporting functions and a headquarters comprised of administrative and communications personnel, form a battalion or regiment. In command is a lieutenant colonel with a major as second-in-command and a regimental sergeant major – they may be regarded as middle managers and they manage 8 – 10 junior managers.*
- *Several infantry battalions, together with armored, artillery, medical, engineering, transport, and workshop units are grouped together as a brigade. In charge are a brigadier general as commander and a colonel as second-in-command, together with a brigade sergeant major. They are to be regarded as senior managers and they supervise a dozen or more middle managers.*
- *A division usually consists of three brigades – together with an extra heavy artillery regiment and other supporting units. The*

commander is a major general with a brigadier general as second-in-command and they, as senior managers, have control over half-a-dozen other senior managers on a lower level.
- *All the managers mentioned above are line managers.*
- *At the brigade and divisional headquarters there are some staff officers with their personnel who deal with logistics, intelligence, training, planning, finances, and stores. These officers are to be regarded as middle managers.*

SOCIAL CONDITIONS OF EMPLOYEES

The last aspect of the working environment that merits attention is the social conditions of workers. Under social conditions, we understand all relationships that impact the workers' performance: family life, participation in the community and the social relationships between workers.

Improving the Working Environment

- ***Social Conditions at Home***

The biggest source of stress in the life of a worker is usually his or her work situation; the second biggest source of stress is the home and the family. If an employee has an unhappy marriage, fights with his or her in-laws, or has constant worries over his or her children then that certainly has a bearing on his or her productivity.

All this stress saps that person's energy and attracts his or her attention away from the work situation.

The result is less than satisfactory work performance, absenteeism, and unnecessary accidents. All these erode a firm's profitability.

The reverse is also true. It has been shown that workers who are happily married and have a healthy family life are usually more satisfied with life in general and with their work in particular. They are, moreover, workers that are usually more productive and their supervisors are more satisfied with their work.

The reason is clear:

o Workers who have a happy family life have less worries and stress than other workers and they can, therefore, dedicate more attention and energy to their jobs; and
o The social support these workers receive at home help them to handle work-related stress more effectively.

It makes sense for management to help workers with family-related stress to receive counseling from a psychologist or a social worker. Such an employee support or assistance program certainly costs something, but, as has been mentioned previously, it pays rich dividends in improved productivity, less absenteeism, and fewer accidents.

- ***Participation in the Community***

Workers do not spend all their time only at home and at work; they usually are also involved with one or more aspects of community life. They are also members of other organizations and associations such as churches, welfare organizations, sports and social clubs, and political parties.

Some employers frown on this participation by their employees in community life. They feel that these activities distract the workers' attention and energy away from their jobs. This is, however, a misplaced notion.

Investigations have shown that workers who are involved with their communities tend to be better workers than those who are not. There is more than one explanation for this state of affairs:

- o In the first place it can be said that a worker who is also a member of a church council or of the committee of a club acquire new skills and knowledge which he or she can transfer to the work situation;
- o Community service brings people into contact with each other who would otherwise not have known each other. In this manner informal networks are formed and these networks and contacts can be utilized profitably in the work situation; and
- o People who are involved in the community receive social support from the people they get to know in this manner. This social support helps people to withstand work-related stress more effectively.

> *I was involved with the church council of a congregation in an industrial town where most inhabitants were employed by the same industrial giant. People from the highest to the lowest levels served on the church council – a plant manager, several senior managers, several supervisors, and some skilled and semi-skilled workers. These people got to know each other in a setting not related to their workplace and it definitely facilitated improved relations between management and the workforce in general. Managers saw workers on the lowest levels as fellow human beings with names and families and not just as numbers. The workers were convinced of the integrity and goodwill of managers. One of the results was a corporate culture where ordinary workers were allowed to talk directly to senior managers outside the work situation.*

It is, therefore, profitable for concerns when their employees are involved in all sorts of community-based organizations. This involvement should, therefore, be encouraged and rewarded. It should count in the favor of a job applicant when he or she is actively participating in community life.

- ***Social Support in the Workplace***

Employees in a certain workplace must know each other. They are required to work together in groups, departments, teams or sections and co-operation is impossible if they remain strangers to each other. The formal relationships in any workplace imply that the workers in question get acquainted with each other.

In a previous section of this chapter, attention has been given to the selection and formation of successful and productive teams. An important by-product of such formal relationships in the workplace is the informal relationships that develop from them.

People who get to know each other in a workplace can also form certain other relationships. When they like each other, they can become friends who spend breaks together, eat together, and even visit each other at home. These social relationships are important spin-offs from the work situation and they can contribute significantly to the amount of work satisfaction a worker experiences.

Such informal relationships and friendships can be beneficial to an organization. When people from different departments know each other well it helps to eliminate or by-pass excessive red tape. These people can communicate directly and informally with each other without using the formal channels and save much time and effort in this manner.

These informal relationships are also an important source of social support. People who share a common workplace understand the type of stress they are all subjected to and can therefore give better emotional support when somebody experiences a stressful spell.

Some employers feel that all forms of "fraternization" between workers or workers and supervisors are to be discouraged since it would take up too much work time when employees chat more than necessary. Of course, workers can indeed waste much time to the detriment of productivity when they socialize too much during work time. On the other hand, productivity can be enhanced when there are many informal networks and friendship groups in an organization.

Chapter 6
Planning for Enhanced Productivity

Chapter outline:
- *Productivity diagnosis*
- *The planning process*
- *A plan of action*

PRODUCTIVITY DIAGNOSIS

After having read this far the reader may easily think that it is a straightforward exercise to reorganize a concern or organization in order to improve the productivity of its workers. After all, all the possible factors influencing productivity have been identified and explained. It is, however, not quite so simple.

An organization consists of a number of human beings who are organized in certain formal and informal relationships. When these relationships are perturbed, unforeseen results may occur. There is usually a certain degree of resistance to any form of change and when the forces of change are strong the reaction may also be strong. Any endeavor at reorganizing an organization must, therefore, be undertaken very carefully and only after extensive investigation and planning. The following pages describe how an organization may be reorganized to boost the productivity of its members, without creating too much disturbances.

- ***Information on Low Productivity***

If you are concerned about productivity in your company, department, or organization and want to do something about it, the first move must be to get some information on low or unsatisfactory productivity. The best place to start is with the financial statements of the last few years. Compare them with the statements of competitive concerns (if these are available). How do your statements look in comparison? Are you profitable enough? Are your operating costs too high?

If you are dissatisfied with the results of your analysis then the chances are that you may have a productivity problem. This information does not, however, pinpoint the source or sources of the problem.

Information on low productivity is also available in the personnel filing system. Any organization that tries to be competitive must have a system for the appraisal of employees as described in the first chapter of this book. It is fairly easy to see how many workers do not perform as expected and to what extent. Identify the workers with whom performance standards have been agreed and who do not deliver on their promises. Compile the necessary statistics to get a comprehensive picture.

- **Sell Your Concerns**

The next step is to make your concerns known and to sell the idea that something must be done about productivity in the organization. If you are the chief executive officer, managing director, or owner of the company then the battle is already largely won because you are the person who makes the decisions. It is important, though, to sell the idea to the workforce. Inform the workers and the unions that an investigation regarding working conditions, the abilities of the workers, and the motivation of the workers is to be undertaken and that their co-operation is very necessary for the investigation to succeed since it will also be in their own interest. They must be invited to tender their thoughts on the subject.

If you are not the boss then you are supposed to sell your ideas to the boss or top management. Compile a memorandum about your findings and buttress your point with appropriate statistics and examples. Make an appointment and present your memorandum in person, explaining the importance of your findings. Ask him or her to study the memorandum and make another appointment a few days later to discuss your conclusions. If your boss or managing director is concerned about the profitability and viability of the concern it will be fairly certain that he or she will be hooked and that he or she will appoint you to undertake or lead the next step – a productivity diagnosis.

It is important to stress that no program for enhancing the productivity of the workforce of a given concern can bear fruits if top management is not backing the program enthusiastically and wholeheartedly. If the boss or the board of directors and the managing director feel uncertain about the necessity to conduct a campaign to improve productivity, it cannot be expected of anyone else in the organization to regard the exercise seriously.

- ***Conducting a Productivity Diagnosis***

There is no standard method for conducting a productivity diagnosis since no two organizations have the same problems. The following steps should, however, lead to satisfactory results:

- ***Conduct Interviews or Convene a Workshop:***

Apart from structured interviews with various key members of the organization and other stakeholders, it may prove worthwhile to convene a workshop of one or two days with a few stakeholders where all the aspects of the organization's functioning are discussed, analyzed, and diagnosed. Such a workshop will ensure that all the participants will accept co-responsibility for any malfunctioning that is uncovered. To ensure maximum participation, the participants can be grouped into syndicates of not more than six members each where various topics may be discussed and reports may be compiled to be presented to the whole workshop.

To ensure the maximum productivity from such a workshop the members must be trained in teamwork, organizational and systems theory, and creative thinking. They ought to be informed of all the factors influencing productivity or the lack thereof – as explained in this book. It must be stressed that the workshop has to do the work and that the identification of problems and their solutions should not come from the facilitator, but from the gathering as a whole.

Prepare a detailed agenda and distribute all documents and reading material a few days before the start of the workshop. That will ensure that all the participants are prepared and know what is expected from them.

- *Compare the Financial Reports of the Organization with the Reports of Competitors:*

This should have already been done, but it may be repeated with a more thorough analysis.

- *Analyze the Work Performances of Workers To Ascertain Whether They Have The Necessary Skills And Competencies For Their Jobs:*

This step should have also been done already, but a more thorough analysis is necessary. Identify the workers, teams, and departments where the problem is worst and compile the necessary statistics. The appraisal reports of workers ought to show whether low productivity results from personality problems, wrong skills, low abilities, wrong behavioral patterns, bad social skills, bad attitudes, or motivational problems. Make sure whether misunderstandings due to cultural differences between supervisors and workers and between workers are not at the root of the problem.

Organize interviews with the workers or teams whose productivity is lowest and talk to them about their skills, qualifications, and training to ascertain their training needs. It may also be necessary to interview the identified workers' supervisors to hear their views.

- *Assess the Level of Motivation of Workers:*

The level of motivation of a workforce or a group of workers is not easy to assess since motivation is an intangible construct. The opinions of a few observant members of the organization, as well as other stakeholders, such as clients, suppliers, and shareholders, may well give an accurate picture of the state of affairs. Interview several key members of the organization who are a representative sample of the workforce – managers, supervisors, workers, trade union officials, and support staff – and ask them to assess the level of motivation. A workshop may be able to uncover interesting facts.

Part of this investigation should be a thorough cultural diagnosis. Those in the know should be able to tell how the workforce as a whole or certain departments view their work, what they see as an acceptable level of productivity and how committed they are to the profitability and prosperity of the firm or organization.

- **Identify Factors which Undermine the Motivation of Workers:**

If it becomes clear that a lack of motivation is part of the problem then it is necessary to identify the factors which undermine the motivation of the workers. Use the issues mentioned in chapter 2 of this book to determine where the choking points lie.

Answers to the following questions ought to be sought:
- How do the workers view the system of incentives of the concern?
- Which psychological needs of the workers are not satisfied in the work situation? Do they receive enough recognition for good work? Do they feel secure or threatened in their positions? Are their jobs interesting and challenging enough?
- Does the work situation provide in the spiritual needs of workers? Are their needs for freedom, responsibility and meaning in life being met?
- How is the example of leaders? Are they inspired and motivated themselves?
- How are the attitudes of employees regarding work in general, the organization, their department or team and their own work?

- What are the prevailing values of the workers? How are these values reflected in the current culture of the organization?
- To what extent are the emotions of the workers respected and taken into consideration?
- Does management and the supervisors have confidence in the abilities of the workers? Do the workers have the self-confidence to perform their work well?
- Are the workers prepared to pay the price in terms of commitment, emotional involvement, effort, time, and energy to meet new productivity standards?
- Which factors are present which might undermine the motivation of workers?
- Are the workers committed to the mission, vision, and goals of the organization?
- Are the workers loyal to the organization, or do they have divided loyalties?

When answers to these questions have been found it ought to be possible to diagnose the problems regarding motivation.

- ***Assess the Morale, Job Satisfaction and Expectations of the Workforce:***

As part of the investigation of the motivation of the workers, the following issues should also be explored: the morale, job satisfaction, and expectations of the workers. Ask the interviewees and the participants to the workshop which remedies they propose for improving the situation; some surprising answers may emerge. Do not under-estimate the resourcefulness and originality of ordinary workers. It is possible that they know the organization better than you expect and when their participation is recruited, they may come with very helpful suggestions and proposals. Beware, though, for proposals which will benefit only the worker or his or her team. Workers may try to misuse the productivity analysis to score some points in the field of organizational politics.

- ***Identify Environmental Factors which May Have a Negative Impact on Productivity:***

It is also necessary to investigate the working environment thoroughly to find any factors which may undermine productivity. Ask the following questions during interviews and during a workshop:

- How are the physical working conditions? Are they safe and comfortable?
- How do the workers view their remuneration? Is it competitive? Do they perceive the reward system as fair?
- How do the workers perceive their chances of advancement and promotion? Do they perceive the system of advancement as fair and equitable?
- How are human relationships in the company? Do managers, supervisors and team members have the necessary social skills? Are all the members treated with respect and is their human dignity recognized? Is conflict and clashes of interest between individuals and groups dealt with in a proper manner?
- How is the culture of the organization? Use the list of issues given in chapter 5 to characterize a corporate culture to get a comprehensive view

of the values, traditions, attitudes, relationships, and stories of the organization.
- Review the policies and practices of the organization – where applicable – with the interviewees. Are these policies and practices appropriate and fair? Do they meet the challenges emanating from the external environment? Do they help to improve productivity in the organization?
- How is the quality of leadership in the organization? Are managers trained to manage, are supervisors trained to supervise and are leaders trained to lead? How is the style of leadership – is it authoritarian or democratic/participative? Are the leaders and managers accessible for the ordinary workers? Do managers know what is going on at grass roots level in the organization? Do managers, supervisors and leaders get the desired results from their inferiors or followers? Do superiors know how to delegate tasks to their subordinates?
- Investigate the shape of the organization: Are the structures designed to be flexible and efficient? Alternatively, is the chain of command rigid and fortified with red tape? Are all the levels of command in the organization necessary, or is the organization over-managed? How efficient is the flow of information? Do the constituent parts of the organization support each other instead of fighting each other? Do a shared vision, common goals, common values,

and common work methods unite the subsystems?
- Investigate the work methods of the organization: How well does the organization succeed in obtaining scarce resources from the environment? How well does the organization adapt to new conditions and changing demands from the environment? Are the demands and needs of clients being met? How fast or how slow does the organization react to new demands and challenges? Are there too many unproductive meetings? Is work being duplicated?
- Is there an effective appraisal system in place? Does management and supervisors know who are the best workers? Does every member of the organization know that his or her good performance is noted and appreciated?
- Investigate the functioning of the whole organization against the following standards: How does the organization's performance in the present compare with its performance at any given moment in the past? How much time is being lost through accidents, bad planning, and inadequate co-ordination between departments and teams? Are there clear boundaries between departments? Is work of a low quality tolerated? How does the organization compare with an ideal state of affairs – i.e. how well is the potential of the organization unlocked?

- How are the social conditions of the workers? Do they have the support of the firm when they experience stress and distress? Do they get social support from co-workers and management? Is there an employee assistance program in place?

It is to be expected that the various stakeholders in the organization (management, employees, clients, suppliers, labor union officials, shareholders, and others) will hold divergent views regarding the issues listed above, since their experience of the organization will be colored by their respective perspectives and since they will evaluate events and trends from different value systems, beliefs, and convictions, expectations and interests. These views and perspectives will have to be compared, verified, and evaluated to come to credible conclusions.

- ***Compiling a Report***

After all the interviews have been conducted and a workshop took place, it is necessary to summarize all the findings in a report. Include all the appropriate statistics. The report should conclude which aspects of work behavior and the make-up of the organization need attention to improve productivity. This report is a necessity, even if you are the boss, since the findings of the productivity diagnosis should be recorded for future reference. If you are not the boss, the report should, of course, be presented to him or her or to the top management. This report should, preferably, be the combined product of the workshop mentioned above. That will ensure that the report will gain in credibility and acceptability.

Recommendations about the following issues should be made:

- Permission to proceed with the planning of the project to improve productivity;
- Personnel or consultants to be assigned to the planning process;
- A proposed budget for the planning process; and
- Special instructions.

THE PLANNING PROCESS

If approval has been given to the proposal to draw up a plan for the improvement of productivity in the organization the next step is to start the planning operation. For this purpose, another workshop should be convened.

> *The need for planning*
> For which of you, desiring to build a tower, doesn't first sit down and count the cost, to see if he has enough to complete it? Or perhaps, when he has laid a foundation, and is not able to finish, everyone who sees begins to mock him, saying, 'This man began to build, and wasn't able to finish.' Or what king, as he goes to encounter another king in war, will not sit down first and consider whether he is able with ten thousand to meet him who comes against him with twenty thousand? Or else, while the other is yet a great way off, he sends an envoy, and asks for conditions of peace (Luke 14: 28 – 32).

There are various elements and stages in the planning process and these must be discussed in sequence:

- ***The Fixing of Goals and Objectives***
Every planning process must have clarity about the objectives and goals that have to be reached. In this case, the objective should be

the improvement of productivity in the organization as a whole or in a certain department or section.

- ***Identification and Analysis of the Problems Encountered***

The results of the productivity diagnosis should be incurporated in the plan that has to be drawn up. The report on the productivity diagnosis must be summarized and analyzed to identify the factors of productivity which need attention.

- ***The Adoption of a Policy***

The rules for the exercise should be formulated. These rules will, inevitably, be taken from the general policies and code of conduct of the organization. The method of decision making, administration, coordinating and control must be decided upon. It is necessary to articulate these rules since a breach of company policy and rules will lead to resistance from several quarters.

- ***Analysis of the External Environment***

All external foctors, which will favor or obstruct the execution of the plan, are to be identified.

o *An analysis of the internal environment:*

All the resources of the organization, which will be at the disposal of the exercise, must be identified, together with the effect they will have on the outcome. Obstacles in the organization which have to be overcome, internal structures and relationships which could have a bearing on the exercise have all to be identified. Ask employees at all levels for suggestions as to how to improve the productivity of the organization as a whole – it is possible that very creative answers will be forthcoming.

- ***The Acquisition of a Strategy:***

The strategy to be used must rest on an analysis of all strengths, weaknesses, obstacles, threats and challenges to the organization. The methods to be used or avoided are to be expounded. The previous chapters in this book contain descriptions of strategies to be followed to remedy certain identified impediments to higher productivity.

- ***Organizing the Participants***

The persons who are to be assigned to run the project must be named – together with each one's qualifcations, experience, and expertise. Their roles, responsibilities and tasks are to be explained. The method of reporting and the frequency of interim reports to top management must be determined.

- ***Budgeting***

The funds allocated to the project have to be divided between different aspects of the exercise.

- ***Formulating a Tactical Plan***

All the practical steps to be taken to solve the identified problems and to counter possible resistance to the project are to be articulated. Each participant's role and tasks must be described. The need for assistance by outside consultants to handle certain aspects of the program (certain training programs, for instance) must be identified. A timetable for action ought to be drawn up; this must include the various phases through which the process has to progress from start to finish.

- ***Methods for Evaluating the Outcomes***

It is necessary to determine how the progress and the end-results of the project are to be evaluated and how feedback will be utilized to adjust and re-adjust goals, strategies, and methods. It is very necessary to evaluate the exercise to ascertain whether the desired results have been achieved. If it transpires that the desired results have not been reached, then the whole exercise, or certain segments of it, must be repeated.

> *When Harmony Gold Mining took over the Elandskraal mine at Randfontein, South Africa, they acquired a mine that made a loss of R41-million during the previous financial year. This unprofitable mine was turned into a profitable enterprise after reorganizing the workforce. Time was taken to draw up a detailed plan and to get the co-operation of trade unions. A key element of this plan was the improvement of productivity. Without this plan, this turnabout would not have been possible.*

It must be kept in mind that an organization is not a mechanism that needs mechanical repairs, but rather a complex organic system that requires careful handling as a whole. It is always possible that the introduction of changes will result in unintended results or even chaos. It is, therefore, all-important to receive feed-back on an ongoing basis to identify and rectify unwanted results before they acquire a life of their own.

> *As a part-time Army chaplain, I visited various military bases. Quite a few displayed this slogan in large letters at a prominent spot:* "IF YOU FAIL TO PLAN YOU PLAN TO FAIL"

A PLAN OF ACTION

After completing the planning process, a detailed plan of action should be the end-result. Such a plan must be in writing and should address the following issues:

- Results of the productivity diagnosis
- Identification and analysis of problems
- A discussion of the present goals, priorities, and objectives of the organization
- Goals, priorities, and objectives that should guide the future development of the organization
- A prediction of future trends and demands that the organization will have to face and satisfy
- Policy statement
- Identification of change agents and their roles
- Identification of departments or sections to be targeted
- Procedures to be followed
- Marketing of the exercise
- Infrastructure and resources available
- Infrastructure and resources needed

Planning for Enhanced Productivity

- Administration and management of the exercise
- Budget and financial management of the exercise
- Specific tasks and assignments
- Phases of the exercise and a timetable for each phase
- Feed-back and evaluation procedures

In any such plan a key role should be assigned to an effective appraisal system. It is impossible to implement a program to improve productivity without a system to monitor the performance of the work force. There must be ways and means to measure improvements in the quality and quantity of work performed, otherwise it will prove impossible to evaluate the success of the program to enhance productivity.

After the plan has been compiled (and approved and adjusted by whomever it must be approved and adjusted) the implementation of the plan can commence.

It is very important to communicate the plan and its objectives as effectively as possible to the whole organization.

This communication process can broadly be divided into five phases:

o The first phase consists of communicating the reasons for the changes that are to take place. It must be expected that many

people will deny that any changes are necessary; according to them, things are fine as they are and changes are superfluous.
- The second phase is to convince the workforce which changes are necessary. A stronger reaction may be expected and active resistance may be encountered. It is necessary to overcome this resistance by an active communication process in which top management ensures everybody of its commitment to the planned changes and in which face-to-face communication by means of meetings, consultations, and interviews take precedence over e-mails, memoranda, notices on the notice board, and articles in the company newsletter. This resistance
- to changes may be compared to a mourning process in which people have to take leave of something to which they have become attached. This resistance is, therefore, fraught with emotions and irrational components and for that reason communication and reassurance on a personal level is so important. This communication may resemble counseling and therapy in certain respects.
- The third phase takes place where the members of the organization start to ask how they will be affected by the changes. When this type of question is being asked – and answered honestly and satisfactorily – a process of adaptation and acceptance is taking place.
- The next phase entails the communication of how the changes will affect every part of the organization. When everybody is informed about the impact, duration, and implications of the proposed changes, further acceptance may be expected.
- The fifth phase occurs where everybody becomes committed to the process and contributes ideas and suggestions about the possible improvement of the plan.

The process of communication should take into account the level of command, seniority, interests, and fears of all those concerned. The message should stress different aspects to technical staff, supervisors, managerial staff, the personnel department, or marketing specialists to target their typical concerns.

It will prove to be worthwhile to identify the natural leaders in the organization and concentrate more on them than on the others. When their commitment has been secured it will be easier to sway the rest of the workforce.

The following principles should be kept in mind while executing the plan after it has been communicated to all interested parties and their commitment has been won:

o Each phase must be completed properly before the next phase can start;
o Later phases rest on previous phases and that means that gains that were made during previous phases should be nurtured and maintained;
o Chaos is always a possibility when changes are being introduced since unexpected results such as industrial action may crop up; to counter that some elements in the organization may try to scrap the productivity plan and revert to old ways;
o Do not implement the plan half-heartedly; the lack of enthusiasm will be contagious and the end-result will be a waste of valuable time and resources;
o Keep all stakeholders in-formed of the progress of the implementation of the plan – transparency is vital;
o Allow all stakeholders to contribute to the process since that will help them to claim ownership of the end-result; and
o The leaders of the process must be credible and legitimate; if they are not trusted, all their moves will be met with mistrust.

Planning for Enhanced Productivity

The process must be monitored and evaluated continuously. The results of each phase must be assessed against the background of the goals, the budget, and objectives of the plan. Do not be discouraged when the new order does not deliver the desired results immediately since that may take time. After all, the stakeholders must re-adjust to new structures, networks, working methods, policies, and practices – and that is not a process that happens easily.

If the evaluation of the program shows that the results have been satisfactory, it does not mean that the productivity management program can be scrapped. After this, it should become an ongoing activity. There will, after all, always be room for improvement. The aim is to make all the members of the organization productivity conscious and to make high productivity a part of the culture of the organization.

It ought to be clear that the productivity battle is a deadly serious battle. It is a battle that must be won since the future of your concern, department, or firm – and ultimately of your country – depends on the outcome. The adversaries are poverty, crime, corruption, hopelessness, nihilism, and degradation. The alternatives to enhanced productivity are mediocrity, stagnation, and corporate death.

This book has explained the rules of the battle as well as

the winning strategies. What is now needed are people who are willing and ready to fight this battle in order to win.

Bibliography

EDITION OF THE BIBLE

Passages from the Bible are quoted from the *World English Bible* as found on a CD with the title *The Bible Collection, Deluxe Edition*, and published by ValuSoft, a division of THQ Inc, Waconia MN, 2002.

LITERATURE

Accel-Team. "Advancing Employee Productivity." Www.Accel-Team.Com.

Adair, J. *Effective Teambuilding*. London: Pan Books. 1986.

Adair, J. *Effective Motivation : How to Get Extraordinary Results From Everyone*. London : Pan Books, 1996.

Allen, D. *Getting Things Done: The Art of Stress-Free Productivity*. London : Piatkus, 2008.

Allan, *Law and Ethics in Psychology*

Anon. "How Productive is SA? The Latest Statistics and Insights." HR Highway, 1(8), : 23–24, Nov/Dec, 2007.

Aminoff, M.J. (*edit.*) *Encyclopaedia of the neurological sciences*. New York : Elsevier Science, 2003.

Ardrey, Robert. *The Territorial Imperative, A Personal Inquiry Into The Animal Origins Of Property And Nations*. London: Collins, 1970.

Argyle, M. *The Social Psychology of Work*. London: Penguin. 1990.

Argyle, M. *The Psychology of Interpersonal Behaviour*. London : Penguin, 1994.

Bain, N. & Mabey, B. *The People Advantage: Improving Results Through Better Selection and Performance*. Basingstok: Macmillan Business, 1999.

Bandura, A. *Self-Efficacy Mechanism in Human Agency*. American Psychologist, 37(2), 122–147, Feb 1982.

Bibliography

Barker, F. *The South African Labor Market*. Pretoria: Van Schaik, 2003.

Barna, G. & Hatch, M. Boiling Point: It Only Takes One Degree : Monitoring Cultural Shifts in the 21st Century. Ventura, Ca: Regal, 2001.

Barnard, A.L. *Motivering en Bestuurspraktyk*. Potchefstroom: Wesvalia, 1991.

Baron, R.A. & Byrne, D. *Social Psychology: Understanding Human Interaction.* Boston : Allyn & Bacon, 1994.

Bly, R.W. *101 Ways to Make Every Second Count: Time Management Tips and Techniques for More Success With Less Stress.* Franklin Lakes, Nj : Career, 1999.

Botha, Z. "20% Blacks at the Top Level : Action Plan To Transform The 'Irish Coffee' Syndrome." Mining Weekly, 7(34), September 7, 2001.

Christopher, W.F. & Thor, C.G. (*Eds*.) *Handbook for Productivity Measurement and Improvement.* Productivity. 1994.

Coens, T & Jenkins, M. *Abolishing Performance Appraisals : Why They Backfire and What to Do Instead.* San Francisco: Berret-Koehler, 2002.

Creamer, T. "The Ironic Tale of Two S African Steel Mills." *Engineering News,* 21(34) : 8-9, August 31, 2001.

Dawkins, *The God Delusion*

Denny, R. *Motivate to Win: Tested Techniques for Greater Achievement*. London: Kogan Page, 1995.

Department Of Employment And Labor Of The Republic Of South Africa. *Industrial Action Report 2023.* Https://Lrs.Org.Za/Wp-Content/Uploads/2024/08/Industrial-Action-Report-2023.Pdf

Dess, G.G. & Picken, J.C. *Beyond Productivity: How Leading Companies Achieve Superior Performance by Leveraging their Human Capital.* Amacom, 1999.

Devenish, G.E. 1999. *A Commentary on the South African Bill of Rights*. Durban: Butterworths, 1999..

Bibliography

Dive, B. *The Healthy Organization: A Revolutionary Approach to People and Management.* London: Kogan Page, 2004.

Encyclopaedia Britannica, "Natural Law". Chicago, Encyclopaedia Brittanica, 2020.

Ennis, S.J. *Manager's Pocket Guide to Interviewing and Hiring Top Performers.* Amherst, Ma : Human Resource Development, 2002.

Esterhuyse, *Sake-Etiek in die Praktyk*

Esterhuyse, Willie. *God En Die Gode Van Egipte.* Wellington: Lux Verbi, 2009.

————. *Sake-Etiek in die Praktyk.* Pretoria: J.L. Van Schaik, 1991.

Fisher, M. *Performance Appraisals.* London: Kogan Page, 1995.

Flood, P. & Gibson, C. *Management and Employment:The Recruitment, Development and Motivation of People.* Kenilworth: Ampersand, 2002.

Frankl, V.E. *The Will To Meaning: Foundations and Applications of Logotherapy.* S.L.: Meridian, 1988.

Gellerman, S.W. *Motivation in the Real World : The Art of Getting Extra Effort from Everyone – Including Yourself.* New York: Dutton 1992.

Goold, M. & Campbell, A. *Designing Effective Organizations: How to Create Structured Networks.* San Francisco: Jossey-Bass, 2002.

Gordon, J.R. *A Diagnostic Approach to Organizational Behavior.* Boston: Allyn & Bacon, 1993.

Harrison, M.I. & Shirom, A. *Organizational Diagnosis and Assessment : Bridging Theory and Practice.* Thousand Oaks: Sage, 1998.

Hesselbein, F. & Johnston, R. *(Eds,.) On High Performance Organisations: A Leader to Leader Guide.* San Francisco: Jossey-Bass, 2002.

Hilliard, V.G. *Performance Improvement in the Public Sector.* Pretoria : Van Schaik. 1995.

Hunter, D, Bailey, A & Taylor, B. *Co-Operacy.* Halfway House: Zebra, 1998.

IMD, "World Competitiveness Scoreboard for 2016." http://www.Imd.Org/Uupload/Imd.Website/Wcc/Scoreboard.Pdf

-----,"World Competitiveness Scoreboard for 2024." https://www.Imd.Org/Centers/Wcc/World-Competitiveness-Center/Rankings/World-Competitiveness-Ranking/Rankings/Wcr-Rankings/#_Tab_List

Jude, B. *The Psychology of Customer Service*. Rivonia: Zebra, 1998.

Kolb, B. & Wishaw, I.Q. *Fundamentals of Human Neuropsychology*. New York: Worth, 2009.

Kowen, M. *How to Recruit your own Staff: An Expert Guide for the Staff-Recruiter and Talent-Hunter*. Johannesburg : Legal Personnel Selections, 1993.

Landman, J.P. "The Number of Days Lost to Strikes Grows with Rising Inequality." *Cape Times, Business Report*, 07.10.2013.

Landy, F.J. *Psychology of Work Behavior*. Pacific Grove: Brooks/Cole, 1998.

Landy, F.J. & Farr, J.L. *The Measurement of Work Performance: Methods, Theory And Applications*. New York : Academic, 1983.

Lennick, D. and F. Kiel. *Moral Intelligence: Enhancing Business Performance and Leadership Success*. Upper Saddle River, NJ: Wharton School, 2008.

Lipsey, R.G. *An Introduction to Positive Economics*. Oxford: Oxford University Press, 1993.

Mafiri, M. I. *Socio-Economic Impact of Unemployment*. Pretoria: University Of Pretoria, 2002 (Dissertation – M.Phil.)

Mann, I. *Managing With Intent*. Cape Town: Zebra, 2002

Marx, Karl. *Communist Manifesto*. New York: Clydesdale, 2018.

Meares, L.B. "A Model for Changing Organizational Culture." *Personnel:* 38–42, July 1986.

Moorhead, G. & Griffin, R.W. *Organizational Behavior: Managing People and Organizations*. Boston: Houghton Mifflin, 1995.

Newstrom, J. & Scannell, E. *The Big Book of Team Building Games: Trust-Building Activities, Team Spirit Exercises, and Other Fun Things to Do*. New York: Mcgraw-Hill, 1998.

Pike, A. *People Risks: A People-Based Strategy for Business Success.* London: Penguin, 2001.

Pinker, Stephen. *The Blank Slate: The Modern Denial of Human Nature.* London: Penguin, 2003.

-----. *How the Mind Works.* London: Penguin, 1997.

Poggioloni, D. "How A R14m Loss was Turned into a R95m Profit in Three Months." *Mining Weekly,* 7(33) : 2-3, August 31, 2001.

Rädel, F E. & Reynders, H.J.J. (*Eds.*). *Inleiding tot die Bedryfsekonomie.* Pretoria : J L Van Schaik, 1988.

Rautenbach, F. *Liberating South African Labor from the Law.* Cape Town: Tafelberg, 1999.

Rhodes, C. *The Office Book: Howlers and Hilarity from the World of Work.* London: Michael O'mara. 2009.

Robbins, S.P. *Organisation Theory: Structure, Design, and Applications.* Englewood Cliffs : Prentice Hall, 1990.

Rothman, S. *Interpersoonlike Vaardighede vir die Bedryfsielkundige.* Potchefstroom: Wesvalia, 1989.

Rothman, S. *Prestasiebeoordeling.* Potchefstroom: PU Vir CHO 1991.

Schein, E.H. *Organizational Psychology.* Englewood Cliffs:Prentice-Hall, 1988.

Shermer, M. *The Believing Brain: from Ghosts and Gods and Conspiracies – How we Construct Beliefs and Reinforce them as Truths.* New York: St Martin's, 2011.

Scholtz, David Adelbert. *Die Voorspelling Van Beroepsukses By 'N Groep Diensdoende Predikante.* Potchefstroom: PU For HE, 1996 (Dissertation – Ph.D.)

Sibiya, H.S. *A Strategy for Allevating Illiteracy in South Africa: a Historical Inquiry.* Pretoria: University uf Pretoria, 2005 (Dissertation Ph.D.)

Singer, Peter. *Ethics in the Real World: 82 Brief Essays on Things That Matter.* Princeton University Press, 2016.

South African Reserve Bank, 2002. Annual Economic Report 2002. Www.Reservebank.Co.Za/Aer

South African Reserve Bank, "Annual Economic Report 2005." Www.Reservebank.Co.Za/Aer

-----, "Annual Economic Report 2006." Www.Reservebank.Co.Za/Publication.Nsf/Ladv
-----, "Annual Economic Report 2007." Www.Reservebank.Co.Za/Publication.Nsf/Ladv
----- "Annual Economic Report 2011." Www.Reservebank.Co.Za/Publication.Nsf/Ladv

Statistics South Africa, General Household Survey 2012: Statistical Release P0318. Http://Www.Statssa.Gov.Za/Publications/P0318/P03182012.Pdf.

Stenger, Viktor *The New Atheism: Taking a Stand for Science and Reason.* New York: Prometheus, 2009.

The Presidency of the Republic of South Africa, *Improving Government Performance: Our Approach.* Pretoria: The Presidency 2010.

Toffler, Alvin. *Power Shift : Knowledge, Wealth and Violence at the Edge of the 21st Century.* London: Bantam, 1991.

Toffler, Alvin. *The Third Wave.* London: Pan, 1981.

Tosi, H.L., Rizzo, J.R. & Carrol, S.J. *Managing Organisational Behavior.* New York : Harper Collins, 1990.

Trading Economics, South Africa Unempoyment Rate 2000–2016. Http://Www.Tradingeconomics.Com/South-Africa/Unemployment-Rate, 2016.

UNISA, SA Labor Productivity at its Lowest in 46 Years. Http://Www.Unisa.Ac.Za/News/Index.Php/2014/01/Sa-Labour-Productivity-At-Its-Lowest-In-46-Years/, 2013.

Veldsman, Theo. *Into the People Effectiveness Arena: Navigating Between Chaos and Order.* Randburg: Knowledge Resources, 2002.

Watling, B. *The Appraisal Check List: How to Help your Team Get the Results you Both Want.* London: Pitman, 1995.

Weiss, T.B. & Hartle, F. *Reengineering Performance Management: Breakthroughs in Achieving Strategy Through People.* Boca Raton: St Lucie, 1997.

World Economic Forum. *Future Of Jobs Report*, January 2025. Https://Www.Weforum.Org/Publications/The-Future-Of-Jobs-Report-2025/

Bibliography

ILLUSTRATIONS

The illustrations used in this book were all downloaded from a CD-ROM published in 2000 by Global Star Software of Mississauga, Canada: *100 000 Designer Clip Art*. The images in this collection are royalty-free.

Chapter 1
The human brain from the outside and the inside
> https://www.researchgate.net/figure/Anatomy-of-the-brain-LEFT-A-side-view-of-the-outside-of-the-brain-showing-the-major_fig1_233887401

South African Constitutional Court Judgment
Pharmaceutical Manufacturers Association of SA and another: In Re Ex Parte President of the Republic of South Africa and Others 2000 (2) SA 674 (CC).

www.ingramcontent.com/pod-product-compliance
Lightning Source LLC
Chambersburg PA
CBHW062015220426
43662CB00010B/1343